First World War
and Army of Occupation
War Diary
France, Belgium and Germany

62 DIVISION
186 Infantry Brigade
Duke of Wellington's (West Riding Regiment)
2/7th Battalion
14 October 1914 - 18 June 1918

WO95/3087/2

The Naval & Military Press Ltd
www.nmarchive.com
Published in association with The National Archives

Published by

The Naval & Military Press Ltd

Unit 10 Ridgewood Industrial Park,

Uckfield, East Sussex,

TN22 5QE England

Tel: +44 (0) 1825 749494

www.naval-military-press.com

www.nmarchive.com

This diary has been reprinted in facsimile from the original. Any imperfections are inevitably reproduced and the quality may fall short of modern type and cartographic standards.

© **Crown Copyright**
Images reproduced by permission of The National Archives, London, England, 2015.

Contents

Document type	Place/Title	Date From	Date To
Heading	WO95/3087-2		
Heading	62nd Division 186th Infy Bde 2-7th Bn Duke of Wellington's Regt 1914 Oct-1918 Jun Disbanded		
Heading	62nd (W.R.) Division 186 Infy Brigade 2/7 Duke of Wellington W Riding Regt 1914 Oct-1916 Dec		
War Diary	Milnsbridge	14/10/1914	08/02/1915
War Diary	Derby	01/03/1915	06/04/1915
War Diary	Doncaster	12/04/1915	14/04/1915
War Diary	Thoresby Park	17/05/1915	30/09/1915
War Diary	Retford	09/10/1915	17/11/1915
War Diary	Newcastle on Tyne	21/11/1915	06/01/1916
War Diary	Larkhill	07/01/1916	13/01/1916
War Diary	New Castle on Tyne	15/12/1915	06/01/1916
War Diary	Larkhill	07/01/1916	07/06/1916
War Diary	Larkhill	17/05/1916	07/06/1916
War Diary	Henham Hall	13/07/1916	13/07/1916
War Diary	Henham	26/07/1916	02/11/1916
War Diary	Bedford	13/11/1916	04/01/1917
War Diary	Southampton	15/01/1917	15/01/1917
War Diary	Havre	15/01/1917	15/01/1917
War Diary	Abbeville	18/01/1917	18/01/1917
War Diary	Frevent	18/01/1917	18/01/1917
War Diary	Rougefay	22/01/1917	22/01/1917
War Diary	Authieule	23/01/1917	23/01/1917
War Diary	Bus-Les-Artois	30/01/1917	14/02/1917
War Diary	Mailly-Maillet	15/02/1917	16/02/1917
War Diary	In The Line K.35.4.0.5 To K.35.B.8.4	17/02/1917	21/02/1917
War Diary	Mailly-Matwood East P.18.A.9.5 Map. 57.D. N.E.	22/02/1917	25/02/1917
War Diary	In The Field Q.6.d.5.8	26/02/1917	26/02/1917
War Diary	Y.Ravine Q.10.d.Q.11.c.Q.11.d.1.8	27/02/1917	28/02/1917
Heading	War Diary 2/7th Battn. Duke of Wellington's Regt 1st March-31st March 1917 Vol III		
War Diary	Beaumont Hamel	01/03/1917	04/03/1917
War Diary	Forceville	05/03/1917	14/03/1917
War Diary	Bois d'Hollande	15/03/1917	15/03/1917
War Diary	Line (L28A)	16/03/1917	18/03/1917
War Diary	Vicinity of Logeast Wood	19/03/1917	24/03/1917
War Diary	Logeast Wood	25/03/1917	31/03/1917
Heading	War Diary 2/7th Duke of Wellington's Rgt. Period 1st April 1917 To 30th April 1917 Volume 4		
War Diary	Henham Place	01/04/1917	01/04/1917
War Diary	Logeast Wood	02/04/1917	02/04/1917
War Diary	York Camp	03/04/1917	04/04/1917
War Diary	Mory	05/04/1917	12/04/1917
War Diary	Line	13/04/1917	18/04/1917
War Diary	Mory	19/04/1917	30/04/1917
War Diary	Henham Place	01/04/1917	01/04/1917
War Diary	Logeast Wood	02/04/1917	02/04/1917
War Diary	York Camp	03/04/1917	04/04/1917
War Diary	Mory	05/04/1917	12/04/1917

Type	Description	From	To
War Diary	Line	13/04/1917	18/04/1917
War Diary	Mory	19/04/1917	30/04/1917
Heading	2/7th Bn. Duke of Wellington's War Diary From:- 1st May 1917 To 31st May 1917 Volume 5		
War Diary	Behagnies	01/05/1917	02/05/1917
War Diary	Line	03/05/1917	03/05/1917
War Diary	Behagnies	04/05/1917	04/05/1917
War Diary	Line	05/05/1917	06/05/1917
War Diary	Mory (B16c5.5)	07/05/1917	07/05/1917
War Diary	Ervillers	08/05/1917	12/05/1917
War Diary	Line	13/05/1917	20/05/1917
War Diary	Courcelles	21/05/1917	29/05/1917
War Diary	Achiet-Le-Petit	30/05/1917	31/05/1917
Miscellaneous	Operation Orders For Attack On A Section Of The Hindenburg Line	01/05/1917	01/05/1917
Miscellaneous	War Diary		
Miscellaneous	62nd Division Order Of The Day	01/05/1917	01/05/1917
Miscellaneous	2/7th Bn. Duke of Wellington's Regt Report on Attack Made on 3rd May 1917	03/05/1917	03/05/1917
Miscellaneous	Orders For Attack By 2/7th Bn. Duke of Wellington's (W.R.) Regiment	13/05/1917	13/05/1917
Heading	War Diary of 2/7th Bn. Duke of Wellington's Regiment From 1.6.1917 To 30.6.1917 Volume 6		
War Diary	Achiet Le Petit	01/06/1917	26/06/1917
War Diary	A Camp I13.c.5.5	27/06/1917	27/06/1917
War Diary	Line	28/06/1917	30/06/1917
Heading	War Diary of 2/7th Bn. Duke of Wellington's Regiment From 1st July 1917 To 31st July 1917 Rendered In Accordance With F.S. Regs. Volume VII		
War Diary	Line	01/07/1917	05/07/1917
War Diary	A Camp I13c.5.5	06/07/1917	08/07/1917
War Diary	A Camp I13b.5.5	09/07/1917	13/07/1917
War Diary	Line	14/07/1917	29/07/1917
War Diary	A Camp I13b55	30/07/1917	31/07/1917
Miscellaneous	2/7th Bn. Duke of Wellington's Regiment. Appendix No.1	09/07/1917	09/07/1917
Miscellaneous	2/7th Bn. Duke of Wellington's Regiment. Appendix No.2		
Miscellaneous	2/7th Bn. Duke of Wellington's Regiment. Appendix No.3		
Miscellaneous	O.C. 2/7th Bn. Duke of Wellington's Regt.	28/07/1917	28/07/1917
Heading	2/7th Bn. Duke of Wellingtons Regt War Diary From 1st August 1917 To 31st August 1917 Rendered In Accordance With F.S Regs Part II Vol VIII		
War Diary	A Camp I13b55	01/08/1917	03/08/1917
War Diary	Line	04/08/1917	05/08/1917
War Diary	Line C.b.c.4.3	06/08/1917	11/08/1917
War Diary	Line	12/08/1917	12/08/1917
War Diary	A Camp Mory	13/08/1917	20/08/1917
War Diary	Mory	21/08/1917	28/08/1917
War Diary	Line	29/08/1917	31/08/1917
Miscellaneous	Battalion Order By Lt. Colonel F. G. Chamberlin M.C. Commanding 2/7th Bn. Duke of Wellington's Regiment	28/08/1917	28/08/1917
Heading	War Diary of the 2/7th Bn. Duke of Wellington's (W.R) Regt. From 1st September 1917 To 30th September 1917 Volume IX		

War Diary	Line	01/09/1917	05/09/1917
War Diary	Mory	06/09/1917	06/09/1917
War Diary	Mory (B 28a. 9.7) (Flynn Camp)	07/09/1917	13/09/1917
War Diary	Line	13/09/1917	29/09/1917
War Diary	A Camp (B28.c.9.7)	30/09/1917	30/09/1917
Miscellaneous	Battalion Orders By Lieut. Colonel F.G. Chamberlin. M.C. Commanding 2/7th Bn. Duke of Wellington's Regiment	05/09/1917	05/09/1917
Miscellaneous	Battalion Orders By Lieut-Colonel F.G. Chamberlin M.C. C de G. Commanding 2/7th Bn. Duke of Wellington's Regiment	12/09/1917	12/09/1917
Miscellaneous	O.C. 2/7th Duke of Wellington's Regt.	29/09/1917	29/09/1917
Miscellaneous	Battalion Orders By Major E.R. Mason M.C. Commanding 2/7th Bn. Duke of Wellington's Regiment.	27/09/1917	27/09/1917
Heading	2/7th Bn. Duke of Wellington's Regiment War Diary 1st October 1917 To 31st October 1917 Volume X		
War Diary	Mory ("A" Camp) B 28 C 97.	01/10/1917	07/10/1917
War Diary	In The Line	07/10/1917	12/10/1917
War Diary	C Camp (N18c4.1)	12/10/1917	30/10/1917
War Diary	Guoy-En-Artois (O19.a)	31/10/1917	31/10/1917
Miscellaneous	Battalion Orders By Major E.R. Mason M.C. Commanding 2/7th Bn. Duke of Wellington's Regiment	06/10/1917	06/10/1917
Operation(al) Order(s)	2/7th Bn. Duke of Wellington's Regt. Order No.5	09/10/1917	09/10/1917
Miscellaneous	Administrative Orders For Move To Beaulencourt Area On 12.10.17 By Lieut. Colonel F.G. Chamberlin M.C. C De G. Commanding 2/7th Bn. Duke of Wellington's Regiment	11/10/1917	11/10/1917
Miscellaneous	Battalion Orders By Lieut. Colonel F.G. Chamberlin. M.C. C De G. Commanding 2/7th Bn. Duke of Wellington's Regiment	29/10/1917	29/10/1917
Miscellaneous	Battalion Orders By Lieut. Colonel F.G. Chamberlin. M.C. C De G. Commanding 2/7th Bn. Duke of Wellington's Regiment	30/10/1917	30/10/1917
Heading	2/7th Bn. Duke of Wellington's Regt. War Diary in Accordance with F.S. Regt. from 1st November 1917 to 30th November 1917 Volume XI		
War Diary	Guoy-En-Artois (O19a)	01/11/1917	11/11/1917
War Diary	Guoy-En-Artois	12/11/1917	13/11/1917
War Diary	Achiet-Le-Petit (Henham Camp)	14/11/1917	16/11/1917
War Diary	Lechelle (P32a.4.1)	17/11/1917	17/11/1917
War Diary	Lechelle	18/11/1917	18/11/1917
War Diary	Bertincourt	19/11/1917	19/11/1917
War Diary	Line	20/11/1917	22/11/1917
War Diary	Havrincourt Wood	23/11/1917	23/11/1917
War Diary	Bertincourt	24/11/1917	25/11/1917
War Diary	Line	26/11/1917	30/11/1917
Miscellaneous	2/7th Bn. Duke of Wellington's Regiment Narrative Of Attacks On 20th And 21st November 1917	20/11/1917	20/11/1917
Map	Bourlon Village		
Miscellaneous	2/7th Bn. Duke of Wellington's Regiment Narrative Of Events From 25th November To Night 3/4th Dec. 1917	27/11/1917	27/11/1917
Heading	2/7th Bn. Duke of Wellington's (W.R) Regiment War Diary Rendered in Accordance with F.S. Regulations From 1st December 1917 To 31st December 1917 Volume 12		
War Diary	Line	01/12/1917	04/12/1917

War Diary	Labucquiere	04/12/1917	04/12/1917
War Diary	Bailleuval	05/12/1917	05/12/1917
War Diary	Goubes	06/12/1917	06/12/1917
War Diary	Tinques	07/12/1917	10/12/1917
War Diary	Lapugnoy	11/12/1917	14/12/1917
War Diary	Busnettes	15/12/1917	18/12/1917
War Diary	Lapugnoy	19/12/1917	19/12/1917
War Diary	Tinques	19/12/1917	31/12/1917
Miscellaneous	Appendix 2 2/7th Bn. Duke of Wellington's Regiment Narrative of Events From 25th November to Night 3/4th December 1917	25/11/1917	25/11/1917
Heading	War Diary of 2/7th Bn. Duke of Wellington's Rgt From January 1st 1918 To January 31st 1918 Volume 13		
War Diary	Tinques	01/01/1918	09/01/1918
War Diary	Maroeuil	10/01/1918	14/01/1918
War Diary	In The Line	15/01/1918	18/01/1918
War Diary	Wakefield Camp	19/01/1918	22/01/1918
War Diary	In The Line	23/01/1918	30/01/1918
War Diary	Wakefield Camp	31/01/1918	31/01/1918
Miscellaneous	Operation Orders By Lieut. Colonel F.S. Thackeray D.S.O. M.C. Commanding 2/7th Bn. Duke of Wellington's Regiment	12/01/1918	12/01/1918
Miscellaneous	Amendment To Operation Orders Of Even Date By Lieut. Colonel F.S. Thackeray D.S.O. Commanding 2/7th Bn. Duke of Wellington's Regiment	12/01/1918	12/01/1918
Miscellaneous	Operation Orders By Lieut. Colonel F.S. Thackeray, D.S.O.M.C. Commanding 2/7th Bn. Duke of Wellington's Regt.	17/01/1918	17/01/1918
Miscellaneous	Operation Orders By Lieut. Colonel F.S. Thackeray, D.S.O.M.C. Commanding 2/7th Bn. Duke of Wellington's Regt.	21/01/1918	21/01/1918
Miscellaneous	Transport officer will make necessary arrangements for collection of water cart at right dump		
Miscellaneous	Operation Orders By Lieut. Colonel F.S. Thackeray D.S.O. M.C. Commanding 2/7th Bn. Duke of Wellington's Regiment	29/01/1918	29/01/1918
Heading	War Diary of 2/7th. Bn Duke of Wellington's Regiment From 1st February 1918 To 28th February 1918 Volume XIV		
War Diary	Wakefield Camp	01/02/1918	01/02/1918
War Diary	Chanticler	02/02/1918	05/02/1918
War Diary	In The Line	06/02/1918	08/02/1918
War Diary	Maroueil	09/02/1918	09/02/1918
War Diary	Monchy Breton	10/02/1918	11/02/1918
War Diary	Tincques	12/02/1918	28/02/1918
Miscellaneous	Operation Orders By Lieut. Colonel F.S. Thackeray D.S.O. M.C. Commanding 2/7th. Bn. Duke of Wellington's Regiment	30/01/1918	30/01/1918
Miscellaneous	Operation Orders By Lieut. Colonel F.S. Thackeray D.S.O. M.C. Commanding 2/7th. Bn. Duke of Wellington's Regiment	31/01/1918	31/01/1918
Miscellaneous	Operation Orders By Lieut. Colonel F.S. Thackeray D.S.O. M.C. Commanding 2/7th. Bn. Duke of Wellington's Regiment	03/02/1918	03/02/1918

Type	Description	Date From	Date To
Miscellaneous	Operation Orders By Lieut. Colonel F.S. Thackeray D.S.O. M.C. Commanding 2/7th. Bn. Duke of Wellington's Regiment	04/02/1918	04/02/1918
Miscellaneous	Operation Orders By Lieut. Colonel F.S. Thackeray D.S.O. M.C. Commanding 2/7th. Bn. Duke of Wellington's Regiment	07/02/1918	07/02/1918
Miscellaneous	Operation Orders By Lieut. Colonel F.S. Thackeray D.S.O. M.C. Commanding 2/7th. Bn. Duke of Wellington's Regiment	09/02/1918	09/02/1918
Heading	62nd Division 186th Infantry Brigade War Diary 2/7th Battalion Duke of Wellington's Regiment March 1918		
Heading	2/7th Bn. Duke of Wellington's (W.R) Regt. War Diary From 1st March 1918 To 31st March 1918 Rendered In Accordance With F.S. Regs Part II Volume XV		
War Diary	Tincques	01/03/1918	02/03/1918
War Diary	Ecoivres	03/03/1918	03/03/1918
War Diary	Line	04/03/1918	09/03/1918
War Diary	Springvale Camp	10/03/1918	15/03/1918
War Diary	Line	16/03/1918	23/03/1918
War Diary	Mont St Eloi	24/03/1918	24/03/1918
War Diary	Duisans	25/03/1918	25/03/1918
War Diary	Line	26/03/1918	31/03/1918
Miscellaneous	(Operation) Order By Major N.A. England, Commanding 2/7th. Bn. Duke of Wellington's Regiment	01/03/1918	01/03/1918
Operation(al) Order(s)	2/7th Bn. Duke of Wellington's (W.R.) Regiment (Operation) Order No.3	02/03/1918	02/03/1918
Operation(al) Order(s)	2/7th Bn. Duke of Wellington's Regiment (Operation) Order No.3	14/03/1918	14/03/1918
Miscellaneous	Recipients Of 2/7th Bn Duke of Wellington's Operation Order No.8	17/03/1918	17/03/1918
Operation(al) Order(s)	2/7th Bn. Duke of Wellington's Regiment (Operation) Order No.8	15/03/1918	15/03/1918
Heading	62nd Division 186th Infantry Brigade War Diary 2/7th Battalion The Duke of Wellington's Regiment April 1918		
War Diary	Souastre	01/04/1918	02/04/1918
War Diary	Pas	03/04/1918	07/04/1918
War Diary	Line	08/04/1918	24/04/1918
War Diary	Bois De Warnemont	25/04/1918	30/04/1918
Operation(al) Order(s)	2/7th Bn Duke of Wellington's Regt Operation Order No.20	23/04/1918	23/04/1918
Operation(al) Order(s)	2/7th Bn Duke of Wellington's Regt Operation Order No.16	10/04/1918	10/04/1918
Operation(al) Order(s)	2/7th Duke of Wellington's Regt. Operation Order No.17	11/04/1918	11/04/1918
Operation(al) Order(s)	2/7th Bn. Duke of Wellington's Regt. Operation Order No.18	12/04/1918	12/04/1918
Operation(al) Order(s)	2/7 Duke of Wellington's Regt Operation Order No.19	17/04/1918	17/04/1918
Miscellaneous	Appendix IV Honours	26/04/1918	26/04/1918
Heading	War Diary of 2/7th Bn. Duke of Wellington's (W.R) Regt. From 1.5.18 To 31.5.18 Rendered In Accordance With F.S. Regulations Part II Vol 17		
War Diary	Bois De Warlimont	01/05/1918	16/05/1918
War Diary	57D NE	17/05/1918	17/05/1918
War Diary	Line 57 DNE	18/05/1918	31/05/1918

Operation(al) Order(s)	2/7th. Bn. Duke of Wellington's Regiment Operation Order No.22		
Operation(al) Order(s)	2/7 Duke of Wellington's Regt Operation Order No.21	23/05/1918	23/05/1918
Operation(al) Order(s)	2/7th Bn. Duke of Wellington's Regiment Operation Order No.26	28/06/1918	28/06/1918
Operation(al) Order(s)	2/7th Bn. Duke of Wellington's Regiment Operation Order No.25	27/05/1918	27/05/1918
Heading	War Diary 2/7th Bn. Duke of Wellington's Regiment From June 1st 1918 To June 18th 1918 Volume XVIII Rendered In Accordance With F.S Regulations Part II		
Map	Map		
Miscellaneous	2/6 Duke of Wellingtons War Diary		
Map	Map		
Miscellaneous	2/6 Duke of Wellington's War Diary (Captured Map)		
Heading	War Diary 2/7th Bn. Duke of Wellington's Regiment From June 1st 1918 To June 18th 1918 Volume XVIII Rendered In Accordance With F.S. Regulations Part II		
War Diary	Map 57DNE Ablainzevelle Line	01/06/1918	02/06/1918
War Diary	Essarts	03/06/1918	06/06/1918
War Diary	Souastre	07/06/1918	15/06/1918
War Diary	Amplier	16/06/1918	18/06/1918
Operation(al) Order(s)	2/7th. Bn. Duke of Wellington's Regiment Operation Order No.27	01/06/1918	01/06/1918
Operation(al) Order(s)	2/7th Bn Duke of Wellington's Regiment Operation Order No.28	05/06/1918	05/06/1918
Operation(al) Order(s)	2/7th. Bn. Duke of Wellington's Regiment Operation Order No.29	09/06/1918	09/06/1918
Operation(al) Order(s)	2/7th Bn Duke of Wellingtons Regt Operation Order No.30	13/06/1918	13/06/1918
Operation(al) Order(s)	2/7th Bn Duke of Wellingtons Regt Operation Order No.31	14/06/1918	14/06/1918

work/3085 (d)

work/3085 (c)

62ND DIVISION
186TH INFY BDE.

2-7TH BN DUKE OF WELLINGTON'S REGT

~~JAN 1917 - JUN 1918~~

1914 OCT - 1918 JUN

DISBANDED

62nd (W.R.) Division
186 Inf. Brigade

2/7 Duke of Wellington
W Riding Regt

1914 Oct — 1916 Dec

WAR DIARY or **INTELLIGENCE SUMMARY**

Army Form C. 2118

Place	Date	Hour	Summary of Events and Information	Remarks and references to Appendices
MILNSBRIDGE	14.10.14	—	LIEUT. COL. R.R. MELLOR TD assumed Command of the 7th (RESERVE) WEST RIDING REGT with a nucleus of 245 N.C.O's & men mostly Home Service Men & medically unfit. The men are billeted at their own homes & attend Drills daily at the following Drill Halls:— MILNSBRIDGE, UPPER MILL, MOSSLEY and LEES.	
— Do —	27.11.14	—	SENT Draft to 7th BN W. RID. REGT Stationed at DONCASTER. Strength:— 128 Men. Conducting Officers:— 2nd LIEUTS BRIERLEY and ROWBOTHAM	
— Do —	11.12.14	—	Battalion marched into Billets at MILNSBRIDGE.	
— Do —	25.12.14	—	By order of G.O.C. Battalion is granted 4 days leave from 25-12-14.	
— Do —	29.12.14	—	Duties resumed after leave.	
1915				
— Do —	1/1/15	—	Draft sent to 7th Bn. W. RID. REGT:— 1 Corpl. 83 men. Conducting Officer 2/Lt C.W. LOCKWOOD	
— Do —	8/1/15	—	The following officers transferred to 7th WEST RD. REGT.:— 2/Lieuts K.C. FISHER-BROWN, J. BRIERLEY, J. HINCHCLIFFE, H.S. NETHERWOOD.	
— Do —	15/1/15	—	Recruiting Party under Command of Major G. TANNER sent to MOSSLEY for one week. Strength 4 Officers, 100 NCO's & Men.	
— Do —	25/1/15	—	Battalion is organized on "Four Company" basis.	
— Do —	3/2/15	—	Draft sent to 9th BN WEST RID REGT: Strength 50 men. Conducting Officer 2/Lt N.T. LAWTON	

Army Form C. 2118

Sheet No 2

WAR DIARY
or
INTELLIGENCE SUMMARY

(Erase heading not required.)

Instructions regarding War Diaries and Intelligence Summaries are contained in F.S. Regs., Part II. and the Staff Manual respectively. Title Pages will be prepared in manuscript.

Place	Date	Hour	Summary of Events and Information	Remarks and references to Appendices
MILNSBRIDGE	5.2.15	—	A detachment of 5 Officers and 226 NCO's & men dispatched to WITHERNSEA for Coast Defence under Command of Captain J. H. CROSSLEY.	
— do —	— do —	—	Designation of Battalion altered from 7th (RESERVE) WEST RID REGT to 27th WEST RID REGT.	
DERBY	1/3/15	—	Battalion moved from Billets MILNSBRIDGE into Billets in DERBY.	
— do —	23/3/15	—	The following were transferred to 2/1st DIVISIONAL CYCLISTS Co:- One Officer (2/Lt H. BARBER) 1 Sergt, 2 Corpls, and 26 men.	
— do —	6/4/15	—	Draft sent to 1/7th WEST RID REGT Strength 4 NCO's 62 men Conducting Officer 2/Lt SC. NORMAN	
DONCASTER	12/4/15	—	Battalion moved from billets in DERBY to the RACE COURSE, DONCASTER, under Canvas	
— do —	13/4/15	—	The following NCO's & men taken on strength from 1/7th WEST RID REGT:- 9 NCO's + 116 men	
— do —	14/4/15	—	The following Officers are taken on strength from 1/7th WEST RID REGT:- Capt G. HAIGH, Lieuts W.R.SYKES, F.E.PHILLIPS, 2/Lieuts W.A. HINCHCLIFFE, J.G. MAISEY	
— do —	20/4/15	—	Battalion armed with the Japanese Rifle and Bayonet	
— do —	12/5/14	—	The detachment of 5 Officers 236 NCO's & men returned to the Battalion from WITHERNSEA	
— do —	14/5/15	—	The following Officers sent to the Home Service Battalion:- 2nd Lieuts W.A. HINCHCLIFFE, C. LAWTON, C.N. BARKER	
THORESBY PARK	17/5/15	—	Battalion moved by MARCH ROUTE from DONCASTER to THORESBY PARK, WORKSOP, 24 miles. 4 Officers and 172 NCO's & men were left behind in DONCASTER to join the Home Service Battalion (27th PROVISIONAL BATTALION)	

WAR DIARY
or
INTELLIGENCE SUMMARY
(Erase heading not required.)

Army Form C. 2118

Sheet 3

Place	Date	Hour	Summary of Events and Information	Remarks and references to Appendices
THORESBY PARK	9/6/15		The following instructional staff attached to the 3/7 WEST RID REGT:— Major G. TANNER, Captain J.H. CROSSLEY and SN Co's.	
— do —	15/6/15		The following officers are struck off the strength and transferred to 1/7 WEST RID REGT, BRITISH EXPEDITIONARY FORCE:— Captain G. HAIGH, 2/Lieuts J.F. BECKWITH, J.G. MAISEY	
— do —	19/6/15		2nd Lieut T.P. BRADBURY is struck off the strength and transferred to 1/7th WEST RID REGT BRITISH EXPEDITIONARY FORCE	
— do —	28/6/15		The Base Detachment transferred to 1/7th WEST RID REGT:— 3 N.C.O's 96 men. Consisting of Officer 2nd Lieut J.H. LAWTON	
— do —	12/7/15		The CHARGER LOADING L.E. RIFLES are withdrawn	
— do —	17/7/15		The following officers struck off the strength & transferred to 1/7th WEST RID REGT:— 2/Lieuts G.W.R. WALKER, J.H. LAWTON	
— do —	31/7/15		The following officers struck off the strength & transferred to 1/7th WEST RID REGT, 2/Lieuts Q.B. HOWCROFT, T.W. BERRY, R.S. PATTEN, W.S. SHAW, J. REYNOLDS, STUFF	
— do —	2/8/15		2/Lieut K.B. MACKENZIE is struck off the strength & transferred to 1/7 WEST RID REGT	
— do —	5/8/15		The following attached to the 2/6 WEST RID REGT at BABWORTH CAMP for training:— 2/Lieuts J.H. CHARLESWORTH 1 S'3 N.CO's 1 men (SIGNALLERS) Lieut C.J. BUTTER AND R.T.H. 2/Lieut N.T. LAWTON Y 3 N.CO's 1 men (MACHINE GUN SECTION)	
— do —	6/8/15		Received draft from 3/7 WEST RID REGT, strength 50 men; several under age and therefore unfit	
— do —	17/8/15		Change of designation 2/1 WEST RID DIVISION will in future be 62ND (WEST RID) DIVISION and 2/1st WEST RID INF Bg DE will in future be 186th INFANTRY BRIGADE	

Army Form C. 2118

WAR DIARY
or
INTELLIGENCE SUMMARY
(Erase heading not required.)

Steel 4

Place	Date	Hour	Summary of Events and Information	Remarks and references to Appendices
THORESBY PARK	21/8/15	—	10 mules taken on the strength.	J.B.
-do-	28/8/15	—	Captain M.E.R. BROCKMAN (Chaplain) attached for rations & accommodation from 20.8.15. C.Q.M.S. J.E. THORP gazetted to the Battalion dated 23/8/15 having reported his arrival and is taken on the strength from that date.	J.B.
-do-	30/8/15	—	Captain H.E. ROBSON R.A.M.C.(T) reports his arrival & is attached from this date. Major H.W. WILLIAMS R.A.M.C.(T) having proceeded to the BRITISH EXPEDITIONARY FORCE is struck off the strength from 27.8.15.	J.B.
-do-	4/9/15	—	40 men transferred from 2/6 WEST RIDING REGIMENT & taken on strength from this date.	J.B.
-do-	7/9/15	—	Sergeant J. VAUGHAN being gazetted to this Battalion as from 17.8.15 & having reported his arrival is taken on the strength from that date.	J.B.
-do-	13/9/15	—	The following lieutenants are gazetted as temporary Captains from 11/5/15 T.M. RUTHERFORD W.V. HAIGH R. JAGGER. The following Lieutenants W.C. POGSON B. SYKES gazetted temporary Lieutenants from 26/8/15.	J.B.
-do-	15/9/15	—	5 Officers and 92 N.C.O's & men left this station for a recruiting tour through the WEST RIDING along with similar detachments from this Brigade.	J.B.
-do-	17/9/15	—	Captain J.H. CROSSLEY having been appointed Adjutant to 3/7 WEST RIDING REGT is struck off the strength of the Battalion as from 9.9.15.	J.B.

Army Form C. 2118

WAR DIARY
or
INTELLIGENCE SUMMARY
(Erase heading not required.)

Instructions regarding War Diaries and Intelligence Summaries are contained in F.S. Regs., Part II. and the Staff Manual respectively. Title Pages will be prepared in manuscript.

Place	Date	Hour	Summary of Events and Information	Remarks and references to Appendices
Thoresby Park	23.9.15	—	2/Lieut T. HAWKSFIELD attached from 11th SERVICE BATTALION is gazetted to this battalion from 19.9.15 taken on the strength. Lieut. F.E. PHILLIPS resigns his commission on grounds of ill health & is struck off the strength from 21-9-15. Lieut. Col. R.R. MELLOR having been transferred to the TERRITORIAL FORCE RESERVE is struck off the strength from the 22.9.15 and the command of the Battalion is taken over by Captain & Adjutant J.S. PEARSON from that date.	
-do-	30/9/15	—	T.H. CHAMBERS and C.Q.M.S. R.G. JOHNSON having been gazetted as from 9/9/15 reported their arrival are taken on the strength of the Battalion from 22/9/15.	
RETFORD	9/10/15	—	BATTALION moved by Route March to Quarters in RETFORD	
-do-	14/10/15	—	Captain & Adjutant J.S. PEARSON hands over command of Battalion to Major N. CHARLESWORTH from this date.	
-do-	17/10/15	—	The Recruiting party Return to this Station	
-do-	18/10/15	—	The undermentioned are attached to this Bn for Rations Accommodation & Discipline.- 2/4th WEST RIDING REGIMENT MACHINE GUN & SIGNAL SECTIONS	
			2/5th " " " "	
			2/6th " " " "	

WAR DIARY
or
INTELLIGENCE SUMMARY

(Erase heading not required.)

Army Form C. 2118

Instructions regarding War Diaries and Intelligence Summaries are contained in F.S. Regs., Part II. and the Staff Manual respectively. Title Pages will be prepared in manuscript.

Place	Date	Hour	Summary of Events and Information	Remarks and references to Appendices
RETFORD	20/10/15	—	CAPTAIN H.J. ROBSON RAMC (T) having proceeded to join the B.E.F. is struck off the strength of this Bn from 19-10-15.	JSB
RETFORD	14/10/15	—	ESTABLISHMENT of Second Line Units reduced to 600 other ranks. Authority G/Gen No 1/5449 (A.G.1) dated 30-9-15.	JSB
—do—	11/11/15	—	From this date the ESTABLISHMENT of OFFICERS is reduced to 23 distributed as follows:— HEADQUARTERS 4 MACHINE GUN OFFICER 1 SIGNALLING OFFICER 1 TRANSPORT OFFICER 1 MAJORS & CAPTAINS 6 SUBALTERNS 10 TRANSPORT OFFICER and half the men of the Transport Section proceed to NEWCASTLE as an advance party preparatory to move.	JSB JSB
—do—	15/11/15			
—do—	17/11/15		LIEUT. W.C. POGSON is appointed BRIGADE GRENADE OFFICER vice CAPTAIN R. JAGGER.	JSB
NEWCASTLE ON TYNE	24/11/15		BATTALION moves by train from RETFORD to NEWCASTLE taking the Quarters previously occupied by the 2/5 DURHAM LIGHT INFANTRY. Previous to moving all First Line Transport, Armoury Equipment,	

Army Form C. 2118

WAR DIARY
or
INTELLIGENCE SUMMARY

(Erase heading not required.)

Instructions regarding War Diaries and Intelligence Summaries are contained in F. S. Regs., Part II. and the Staff Manual respectively. Title Pages will be prepared in manuscript.

Place	Date	Hour	Summary of Events and Information	Remarks and references to Appendices
NEWCASTLE ON TYNE	24/11/15		and Ordnance Stores were handed over to the 2/5 DURHAM LIGHT INFANTRY - Riding Horses and personal equipment taken with the Battalion to NEWCASTLE. The Battalion takes over the corresponding stores & transport equipment from the 2/5 DURHAM LIGHT INFANTRY in NEWCASTLE. All attached men from 2/4, 2/5 & 2/6 WESTRIDING REGIMENT are returned to their respective units on arrival at NEWCASTLE.	JB
-do-	7/12/15		MAJOR G TANNER appointed OFFICER COMMANDING ADMINISTRATIVE CENTRE of the 7th WEST RIDING REGIMENT MILNSBRIDGE is struck off the strength of the Bn from 6/12/15 whilst holding this appointment.	JB
-do-	10/12/15		SECOND LIEUTENANT B.C. JOHNSON is transferred to 3/7 WEST RIDING REGIMENT & is struck off the strength of the Bn from the date. Authority A/14516/630/1.	JB
-do-	10/12/15		SECOND LIEUT. B.C. JOHNSON is attached to this Bn from this date.	JB

WAR DIARY
or
INTELLIGENCE SUMMARY

(Erase heading not required.)

Army Form C. 2118

Place	Date	Hour	Summary of Events and Information	Remarks and references to Appendices
NEWCASTLE-ON-TYNE	15/12/15		All combatant officers to be Medically Examined as to their fitness for Service abroad. J.H.C.	
"	22/12/15		Commenced to dig New Entrenched line for Defence of NEWCASTLE-ON-TYNE. J.H.C.	
"	31/12/15		All documents, lamps etc relative to the NORTHERN COMMAND SCHEME for the CONTROL of MOTOR VEHICLES handed over to 186th INF BRIGADE HQRS. 2nd LIEUT. B.C. JOHNSON having joined B.E.F is struck off the strength of the BATTALION from this date. J.H.C.	
"	4/1/16		The work of digging the NEW ENTRENCHED LINE for the Defence of NEWCASTLE-ON-TYNE is stopped from this date. Lieut W.B. SYKES and 20 other ranks employed by Advance party connecting NEW E-ON-TYNE to AMESBURY (LARKHILL.) J.H.C.	
"	5/1/16		10-20 Train from NEW E-ON-TYNE to AMESBURY by All Battalion heavy baggage loaded	
"	6/1/16		The battalion marched from NEWCASTLE-ON-TYNE to the OLD CATTLE DOCK at 7-10pm and 9-40pm two trains leaving the OLD CATTLE DOCK at 7-10pm and 9-40pm respectively. Arrived at No P CANADA LINES, LARKHILL 1-35pm 7/1/16. All graftos located in NBLE were handed over to the 70th PROVISIONAL BATTALION.	
LARKHILL	7/1/16		LIEUT HEPPENSTALL R.A.M.C (T) is attached to this unit.	
"	13/1/16		The following officers are promoted Temporary LIEUTENANTS, dated 10/11/15. 2/LTS C.W. LOCKWOOD N.T. LAWTON J.H. CHARLESWORTH	

WAR DIARY
or
INTELLIGENCE SUMMARY

(Erase heading not required.)

Army Form C. 2118

26

Place	Date	Hour	Summary of Events and Information	Remarks and references to Appendices
NEWCASTLE-ON-TYNE	15/12/15		All Combatant Officers to be Medically Examined as to their fitness for Service abroad. J.H.C.	
"	22/12/15		Commenced to dig New Entrenched Line for Defence of NEWCASTLE-ON-TYNE. J.H.C.	
"	31/12/15		All documents, lamps etc relative to the NORTHERN COMMAND SCHEME for the CONTROL of MOTOR VEHICLES handed over to 166th INF. BRIGADE HQRS. 2nd Lieut. B.C. JOHNSON having joined the B.E.F. is struck off the strength of the Battalion from this date. J.H.C.	
"	4/1/16		NEW ENTRENCHED LINE for the Defence of the north of NEWCASTLE-on-TYNE is copied from this date by J.O. Advance party consisting Lieut. B. STKES and 20 other ranks moved by 10-28 train from NEWCASTLE-on-TYNE to AMESBURY (LARKHILL). J.H.C.	
"	5/1/16		All Battalion heavy baggage loaded.	
"	6/1/16		The Battalion moved from NEWCASTLE-on-TYNE to AMESBURY by two trains leaving the OLD CATTLE DOCK at 7·10 p.m and 9·40 pm respectively. Arriving at No 8 CANADA LINES, LARKHILL 1·35 p.m 7/1/16	
LARKHILL	7/1/16		All quarters located in N.C.E. were handed over to the 70th PROVISIONAL BATTALION.	
"	13/1/16		LIEUT. HEPPENSTALL R.A.M.C.(T.) is attached to this unit. The following Officers are promoted Temporary LIEUTENANTS, dated 18/11/15. C.W. LOCKWOOD. N.T. LAWTON. J.H. CHARLESWORTH.	

2/LTS   C.W. Lockwood   N.T. Lawton   J.H. Charlesworth

WAR DIARY

or

INTELLIGENCE SUMMARY

(Erase heading not required.)

Army Form C. 2118

Instructions regarding War Diaries and Intelligence Summaries are contained in F.S. Regs., Part II. and the Staff Manual respectively. Title Pages will be prepared in manuscript.

Place	Date	Hour	Summary of Events and Information	Remarks and references to Appendices
LARKHILL	17/1/16		CAPTAIN. H.R. MAUNSELL 2"Bn SHROPSHIRE LIGHT INFANTRY is posted to this battalion for light duty and takes over Command & Payment of 'A' Company from this date.	
"	11/2/16		CAPTAIN W.G. BAGNALL transferred to Territorial Force Reserve and is struck off the strength of the battalion accordingly.	
"	10/3/16		Lieut J. Haden, 2ᵈ LIEUT E TANNER transferred to this battalion from the 3/7 (A DUKE OF WELLINGTONS REGT. and taken on the strength of the battalion.	
"	28/3/16		LIEUT-COLONEL D.F. CAMPBELL D.S.O. takes over command of this battalion vice MAJOR M. CHARLESWORTH, from this date posted to this battalion.	I
"	31/3/16		710 ARMY RESERVE CLASS B RECRUITS posted to this battalion now in Appendix I.	
"	5/4/16		Establishment of battalion on dates specified in accordance with WAR ESTABLISHMENTS PART VII 1915. Authority War Office letter 79/8842 (S.D. 2). C.R.S.O. 114291 (A.4.)	
"	15/5/16		The Battalion marched as part of a RIGHT FLANK GUARD from to PEWSEY from LARKHILL and also billets for the night were occupied at SHARCOTT, 1 mile SW from PEWSEY (Pt "1" QS 282) (N.B. The only men who took part in this march were the "trained men", the Recruits were left behind in camp to continue their recruits training.	
"	16/5/16		The Battalion marched from Pewsey to Devizes where they were in billets for the night.	

WAR DIARY
or
INTELLIGENCE SUMMARY

Army Form C. 2118

Place	Date	Hour	Summary of Events and Information	Remarks and references to Appendices
LARKHILL	17/1/16		CAPTAIN. F.H.R. MAUNSELL 2nd Bn. SHROPSHIRE LIGHT INFANTRY posted to this battalion for Light-Duty and takes over command & Payment of "A" Company from this date.	
"	11/1/16		CAPTAIN W.G. BAGNALL transferred to Territorial Force Reserve and is struck off the strength of this battalion accordingly.	
"	10/3/16		Lieut J. Maden 2nd Lieut E. TANNER transferred to this battalion from the 3/1 DUKE OF WELLINGTONS REGT. and taken on the strength of the battalion.	
"	28/3/16		LIEUT. COLONEL D.F. CAMPBELL D.S.O. takes over command of the battalion vice MAJOR M. CHARLESWORTH from this date.	
"	31/3/16		710 ARMY RESERVE CLASS B RECRUITS posted to this battalion on dates specified in Appendix I in accordance with establishment of battalion now in accordance with WAR ESTABLISHMENTS PART VII 1915 Authority War Office letter 79/8642 (S.D.2) C.R.S.O. 11429 (A.H.)	I
"	5/4/16		The battalion marched as part of a RIGHT FLANK GUARD from LARKHILL and did billets for the night were occupied at SHARGOTT South West from PEWSEY. (A/c 1" OS 282) (N.B. The only men who took part in this march were the "trained men" the Recruits were left behind in camp to continue their recruits training.	
"	11/5/16		The Battalion marched from Pewsey to Devizes where they were in billets for the night.	

WAR DIARY
or
INTELLIGENCE SUMMARY
(Erase heading not required.)

Army Form C. 2118

Instructions regarding War Diaries and Intelligence Summaries are contained in F.S. Regs., Part II. and the Staff Manual respectively. Title Pages will be prepared in manuscript.

Place	Date	Hour	Summary of Events and Information	Remarks and references to Appendices
Larkhill	17/5/16		The Battalion marched from Jerript to Trowbridge where they were in billets for the night.	
"	18/5/16		Battalion marched from Trowbridge to Little Cheveral where they were billeted for the night.	
"	19/5/16		The Battalion marched from Little Cheveral back to quarters at Larkhill arriving there at 2.30 p.m.	
"	1/6/16		The Battalion moved from Larkhill to Henham Hall, nr Wangford, Suffolk by three trains leaving Amesbury Station with detaining at Halesworth. Arrival at Henham Station. The Battalion went under canvas at Henham. Halesworth 3 a.m.	
Henham Hall	1st-4th/6/16 5/6/16		The Battalion marched to Ockestone St Marys arriving there 5 p.m. where they billeted for the night.	
"	6/6/16		The Battalion relieved the 1/5 Bn Duke of Wellington Regt in the trenches at The Custard at 10 p.m. During the night they had parties of 1. Listening Post, 2. Wiring, 3. Raids 4. Listening Post.	
"	7/6/16		The Battalion left the trenches and marched back to Larkhill, arriving there at 3.30 p.m.	
Henham Hall	13/9/16		The Battalion left hut in a Brigade route march via Wangford-Uggshall-X Roads East of Stoven - Junction South West of Wangford and back to camp.	

1875 Wt. W 593/826 1,000,000 4/15 J.B.C. & A. A.D.S.S./Forms/C. 2118.

WAR DIARY or INTELLIGENCE SUMMARY

Army Form C. 2118

Place	Date	Hour	Summary of Events and Information	Remarks and references to Appendices
Larkhill	17/5/16		The Battalion marched from Larkhill to Trowbridge where they are now billeted for the night.	
	18/5/16		Battalion marched from Trowbridge to Little Cheverel where they are billeted for the night.	
	19/5/16		The Battalion marched from Little Cheverel back to Larkhill arriving there at 2.30 p.m.	
	11/6/16		The Battalion marched from Larkhill to Hexham Hall, near Wanford, Suffolk by three Trains leaving Amesbury Station. The detraining at Halesworth. Arrived at Hexham Hall, Halesworth 3 a.m. The Battalion went under canvas.	
	2/7/16 5/6/16		The Battalion marched to Oulton where they were there 5 p.m. when they bivouacked for the night. The Battalion relieved the 4/5 Bn Duke of Wellington Regt in the trenches at The Bluff at 10 p.m. During the night they had further 1 Officer & Warrng & Rains 4 Int'ce Repts.	
	7/6/16		The Battalion left the trenches and marched back to Larkhill arriving there at 3.30 p.m.	
Hexham Hunt	13/6/16		The Battalion Cpt. had a Brigade route march near Wangford, Wyrdale – X roads East of Station – further Cross West of Wangford – back to Camp	

Army Form C. 2118

WAR DIARY
or
INTELLIGENCE SUMMARY

(Erase heading not required.)

Instructions regarding War Diaries and Intelligence Summaries are contained in F.S. Regs., Part II. and the Staff Manual respectively. Title Pages will be prepared in manuscript.

Place	Date	Hour	Summary of Events and Information	Remarks and references to Appendices
HENHAM	26/7/16	—	The battalion marched to WORLINGHAM (Nr BECCLES) where they marched past HIS MAJESTY KING GEORGE V marching first in Column of Fours. First time therefore did not attend this parade.	
"	4/9/16		Lieut Colonel D.F. CAMPBELL. D.S.O. M.P. died at 1.0 a.m. He was taken ill on Sunday Aug 3rd 1916, admitted to COTTAGE HOSPITAL SOUTHWOLD September 2nd 1916 and died on the above date suffering from HAEMATIMIOIS. He is struck off the strength of the battalion from this date.	
	5/9/16		Memorial Service for the late Lieut. Col. D.F. Campbell D.S.O. G.O.C. Division attended.	
	9/9/16		Captain J.E. Martin R.A.M.C. arrives & attached for duty with this battalion vice Captn Knox into hospital with fever.	
	17/9/16		Brigade Operations carried out by Lionmouth with Blythburgh Common. The attack practised. 2/Lieut E.H.D. Walker is transferred from the 3/6 Duke of Wellington Regt taken on the strength of this battalion dated 7/9/16.	
	20/9/16		Major W. Chadwick attached a Course of Instruction (Lewis) Hythe commences 26.9.16	
	22/9/16		Lieut Col. H.Clifford D.S.O. having assumed 2/5 Yorks Lancs (& Major) is taken on the strength battalion 10 D. Cory dated 7/9/16.	
	30/9/16		Practice Memorial Drill Southwold Common. Inspection by G.O.C. K. Army.	
	4/10/16		Inspection by General Sir Pinhe Hamilta Homeforces Southwell Common.	

WAR DIARY
or
INTELLIGENCE SUMMARY

Army Form C. 2118

Place	Date	Hour	Summary of Events and Information	Remarks and references to Appendices
HEYTHAM	26/7/16	-	The battalion marched to WORLINGHAM (Nr BECCLES) where they would greet HIS MAJESTY KING GEORGE V marching past in Column of fours. That same Ecourf't did not attend this ceremony as he was taken ill on	
"	4/9/16		Lieut Colonel D.F. CAMPBELL D.S.O. M.P died at 1.0am on Sunday Aug 3rd 1916, admitted to COTTAGE HOSPITAL SOUTHWOLD September 2nd 1916. The above date suffering from HAEMATITIS. He is struck off the strength of the battalion from this date	
	5/9/16		Memorial Service for the late Lieut Col. D.F. Campbell D.S.O. G.O.C. Division attended	
	9/9/16		Captain G.E. Martin R.A.M.C arrived & attached for duty vice Captain Keay into hospital ill. Seven.	
	17/9/16		Brigade Operations carried out by the most with Brighthorpe. Command the attack practised	
			2/Lieut E.H.D. Watkin is transferred for the S/6 Border Regt. to take on the strength form between dates 7/9/16	
	20/9/16		Major M. Chadwick attached a Course of Instruction (Senior) at Hythe commencing 26.9.16	
	22/9/16		Lieutcol Stopford D.S.O having arrived to 7/5 Yorks Lanes (& Major) is taken on the strength pursuant to D Corps orders 29/9/16	
	30/9/16		Practice Memorial Drill Southwold Common. Inspection by G.O.C. h. Army	
	4/10/16		Inspection by General Bruce Hamilton Commander Southward Coast	

WAR DIARY or INTELLIGENCE SUMMARY

Army Form C. 2118

Place	Date	Hour	Summary of Events and Information	Remarks and references to Appendices
Hunham	18.10.16		Lieut. J.R. Rowbotham took over command of Battalion transport vice Lieut. C.W. LOCKWOOD. Dated 6.10.16. S/H.	
"	25.10.16		Capt. W. GRAHAM took over 2nd i/c during absence of Major M. CHARLESWORTH. S/H.	
"	2.11.16		Battalion move to Bedford 2.11.16 with the Division. S/H.	
Bedford	13.11.16		Capt. G.H. LOCKWOOD returned to duty with 3rd Line. Dated 19.11.16 S/H.	
"	14.11.16		The Battalion commenced to fire the General musketry course at Harrowden Range 18.11.16. S/H.	
"	21.11.16		Capt. W. GRAHAM visited the Army in the Field. Dated 14.12.16. S/H.	
"	2.12.16		2/Lieut. E.G. HARRIS appointed Adjutant vice Major J.S. PEARSON. dated 11 or 4/19/16. S/H.	
"	3.12.16		Lieut. S.C. WORMALD transferred to 6th Res. Bn. W. Regt. Clipstone. Dated 3.12.16. S/H.	
"	4.12.16		Capt. 8 H. WATSON took command of "A" Company. dated 4.12.16. S/H.	
"	5.12.16		2/Lieut. S.N. MILNES having reported from Clipstone is taken on strength dated 4.12.16 vice Lieut. S.C. WORMALD. S/H.	
"	18.12.16		MAJOR. J.S. PEARSON proceeded to Grove Park S.E. for three weeks course with A.S.C. M.Y. S/H.	
"	2.1.17		Capt. G.E.G. COCKBURN M.C. 2nd Royal Irish Fusiliers joined for duty with the Battalion. Dated 2.1.17. S/H.	
"	5.1.17		Battalion finished the Grub. S/H. Weather was generally during the course S/H.	
"	26.12.16 to 4.1.17		Lewis Gunners commenced to fire their course and finished on 4.1.17. S/H. Firing from the hip practice both with Lewis Gun & rifles at Harrowden Range. Weather very cold & a good deal of rain. S/H.	

2/7 W Riding

WAR DIARY
or
INTELLIGENCE SUMMARY
(Erase heading not required.)

Army Form C. 2118

Instructions regarding War Diaries and Intelligence Summaries are contained in F.S. Regs., Part II. and the Staff Manual respectively. Title Pages will be prepared in manuscript.

Place	Date	Hour	Summary of Events and Information	Remarks and references to Appendices
Bedford	15.1.17	6.0 am	Entrained at BEDFORD for SOUTHAMPTON.	
Southampton	—	5.30 pm	Embarked at SOUTHAMPTON for LE HAVRE. Sailed 11.30pm.	
Havre	—	11.12 pm	Arrived LE HAVRE and disembarked, marched to REST CAMP No 1, stayed two nights, marched off at 9.0 am 17th inst for entrainment at Point 3. Separated from here at 1.30 pm – 5 miles each way from 7th Rest Camp.	
Abbeville	18.1.17	9.0 pm	Arrived ABBEVILLE, orders for next Station given – FRÉVENT.	
Frévent	18.1.17	10.00 am	Arrived FRÉVENT – marched to ROUGEFAY – 4 miles, arrived at 3.30 pm – stayed in billets until 22.1.17. Weather very bad since leaving England.	
Rougefay	22.1.17	10.30 am	marched to AUTHIEULE – 14 miles – arrived 6.30 pm 5th Billeted.	
Authieule	28.1.17	10.0 am	marched to BUS-LES-ARTOIS – 10 miles. Billets in remainder. Weather very bad. Pte S 2/17 38.	
Bus les Artois	30.1.17		Capt G.E.G. COCKBURN, M.C. promoted Major. London Gaz the Jan 2, 1917 on 2/1/17 8/2 Lewis Gun Hand Carts to be withdrawn & limbered G.S. wagons substituted.	
Bus les Artois	31.1.17			
"	22.1.17		All Officers proceeded to 96 and 97 Ind Bdes for instruction in the trenches.	
"	31.1.17		Lieuts. GLORG, BEAUMONT, HODGSON and CHARLESWORTH attached to 3rd Army for 6 days Course of Instruction in Grenades. Capt Rutherford, WATSON, KNOCKER attached to 3rd Army for instruction in Grenades 9th	

W. Clifford Lieut Col
1/7th Duke of Wellington Regt

Original VOLUME II

Army Form C. 2118

WAR DIARY or INTELLIGENCE SUMMARY

2/7th DUKE OF WELLINGTON REGT

(Erase heading not required.)

Instructions regarding War Diaries and Intelligence Summaries are contained in F.S. Regs, Part II. and the Staff Manual respectively. Title Pages will be prepared in manuscript.

Place	Date	Hour	Summary of Events and Information	Remarks and references to Appendices
BUS-LES-ARTOIS	1.2.17		GENERAL ROUTINE. Regt in HUTMENTS providing working parties.	
"	2.2.17		ROUTINE. same location	
"	3.2.17		"	
"	4.2.17		2/Lt. E.G. HARR'S was chd pt of M.G.I. succeed by 2/Lt. H. Hungerford. Actg. Maj.	
"	5.2.17		SMALL BOX RESPIRATOR minute inspection & demonstration.	
"	6.2.17		PROVIDING working parties.	
"	7.2.17 8.2.17		(Wkrs) A.} Coys went to TRENCHES at HEBUTERNE. K.17. (K.3.-M.22) A. Coy B. Coy 58 Bde B.} period 24 hrs in that line 56 Suttee sb Bde Pte. HAGGERTY A. B. Coy. wounded.	min West
"	8.2.17 9.2.17		(Wkrs) C.} Coys relieved A. & B. Coys. in same location D.} same period. CASUALTIES:- NIL.	
"	9.2.17		GENERAL. REGL. ROUTINE. Finding working parties.	
"	10.2.17		"	
"	11.2.17		"	2/Lt. E.G. Ilanut took over duty o.c. Bomb Boot Store on vacation by 2/Lt. H. ORMEROD went to ST RIQUIER to 3rd ARMY SNIPING Course.
"	12.2.17		GENERAL R. ROUTINE. Adjut and was on n.7.ev.4. Majr. E.G. CHAMBERLIN The Water Regt. joined t.a.d w.o. Letter 6576 The Regt. as 2nd in Majr. Weather exceedingly cold. Hard frost. Regt A.G.G.A. Standing To. to move into the LINE. K.3-M.22. (T.Maj) K.35.A.0.5.10.K.33.B.8.4 inclusive. Moved to MAILLY-MAILLET. Billet No. 79. Majr. Cock taken	A.G.G.A. went up to inspect 2nd LINE system of the part of the pay 2/7 A.m. finding working parties. Plague of rats in Billet M.O. killed 151 m (this the m r.c.) whilst asleep.
"	13.2.17		"	

WAR DIARY or INTELLIGENCE SUMMARY

Army Form C. 2118

Place	Date	Hour	Summary of Events and Information	Remarks and references to Appendices
BUS.LES ARTOIS	14.2.17		Weather brightly cold, but clear. Nth. easterly wind prevailing. - GENERAL REGL. ROUTINE. Regl. in HUTMENTS. Finding working parties. - Received orders to move to MAILLY-MAILLET billet No. 79. arrived & have taken it over 6 P.M. Major Cook burn & Coy officers with our 3 battalion each proceeded to WHITE CITY to reconnoitre the position as far as provided 7 p.m.	
MAILLY-MAILLET	15.2.17		Thaw set in. everything as sticky as it could be. Mud very bad. Visited by the Div. GENL. - MAJOR GENL. N. BRAITHWAITE. Bichlub Toni - Day spent preparing to move up.	
"	16.2.17		REGL. ROUTINE. Finding fatigue parties. More proper to send up to reconnoitre our position -	
In Tht LINE K.35. A.0.5 K.35. B.9.4	17.2.17.		Moved up to WHITE CITY & took over LINE from K.3 - M.22 (T.Map) from K.35.A.0.5 to K.35.B.9.4 at 3. p.m. No trenches at all, line of posts in SHELLHOLES. A/B. Coys inclusive C.D. Coys front POSTS. SUPPORT. Relief effected by 6.15. A.M. 18.2.17. Regl. Relieved 7/0. D. of W. (W.R) Regl. Major. CHAMBERLIN took over Adjty. vice ADJT. (A) sick.	A. Coy.:- BRASS MONKEY. TIGER. POIND. 34. LEOPARD'S SPOT B. Coy.:- R.M.T. GOATS-HORN. MOUSE. SKUNK. HEDGEHOG TRENCH B. Coy.:- LEGEND TRENCH. BLIND PIG. DUN COW. BIRD. PARROT. PIGEON.
"	18.2.17.		IN THE LINE. Conditions could not have been worse. men quite cheery. Taking the spirited breaking-in to trench life very well. Reconnoitering & skillful movement by day to have visited.	
"	19.2.17.		Usual trench routine. A Coy relieved by C. Coy. - B. Coy relieved by D. Coy. successfully effected under adverse conditions, mud & weather.	

WAR DIARY
or
INTELLIGENCE SUMMARY

Army Form C. 2118

Place	Date	Hour	Summary of Events and Information	Remarks and references to Appendices
IN THE LINE K.33.A.0.5 K.32.B.8.4.	20.2.17		Usual Trench routine. Major Coe to hurry round & forward to M.M. BARWOOD order to see about Billets. Regt coming out. C.O. knocked out, remaining to carry on.	
"	21.2.17		Usual Trench routine. Regt relieved by 21/2 Bn. (S) The Manchester Regt under Col. NORMAN (2nd in Comd Army) V.G. Regt) Relief completed by 6.0 A.M. C.O. & 1 Sergt remained till R. Coys W.O. Casualties during tour of duty (4 days) – decorated 1 man killed. 22.2.17	
HAPLY-MA T WOOD EAST. P.18.A.9.5. MAR.5.D. N.E.	22.2.17		Regt in Huttments. Day spent in resting & generally cleaning up. Major Coe taken to hospital. No.29. GEZANCOURT. Inspections. DIV. GEN'L wounded came round inspected the Regt. 2/Lt.A.H.ORMER O.D. reporting in. Taken on as SNIPING INTELLIGENCE OFFICER. EVERYONE now issued with ... antigas ...	
"	23.2.17		Regt in Huttments. Major T.G. CHAMBERLIN acptd. actg. 2nd in Comd. vice Major G.E.G. Creek Baron evacuated sick. Regt R. ... this picture. Brig. GEN'L HILL C.B. C.M.G. D.S.O. came round visited the C.O. making 126. INF. Brig. very careful & thorough inspection road points concerning the health team but of the men. LOUSES in equipment etc. Brigade Major. Major R. BOYD.S.O.	
"	24.2.17		Regt in Huttments. Day spent in inspection by setting out necessary incidents. C.O. + 2/in Cmd. went to Brigade Con'fe at FORCEVILLE. 2/Lt. H. FURNESS + 2/Lt. H. ROWBOTHAM returned from Hospital. 2/Lt. S.J. CLAPHAM returned from T.M. COURSE. B. Coy	

Army Form C. 2118

WAR DIARY
or
INTELLIGENCE SUMMARY
(Erase heading not required.)

Place	Date	Hour	Summary of Events and Information	Remarks and references to Appendices
MAILLY-MAILLET WOOD EAST R.18.A.9.5 Map57.D.N.E	25.2.17		Reg'tl HUTMENTS. Received orders to stand by to move at 30 mins notice. S.A.M. Did not materialise till 6 P.M. Had a test move at 10.30. A.M. Beautiful day of weather. Reg'l routine in afternoon. - Moved at 6 p.m. to report to 187. 2nd Inf. Bde. at Q.17.A.8.8. Bn. stood by to support Bn. 187. 2nd. Bde. which was to attack 6 A.M. x Post, and An. rested all night on side of the road. Q.16.D.5.8.	
"	26.2.17			
IN THE FIELD Q.16.d.5.8.	26.2.17	At 6.15 A.M. Battalion - STOOD TO - to move at 15 min notice. Then fresh orders rec'd. to STAND TO - till 12 NOON. Eventually moved in DUG-OUTS in Trenches in Y'RAVINE		
		Q.10.d. Q.11.c. A.C.D Coys	Q.11.d.1.8 Hd. Qrs	Q.11.d.1.8 B. Coy	on MAP. K.3-M.22. GENERAL SALVAGE OPERATIONS and WORKING PARTIES commenced	
Y. RAVINE Q.10.d. Q.11.c. Q.11.d.1.8	27.2.17		Reg'l. Rout ine. G.S.O as above. W.P.	
"	28.2.17		Reg'l. Rout ine G.S.O as above W.P.	

Clifford Lt.Col
2/7 Duke of Wellington's
6 (W.R) Regt

3-3-1917.

ORIGINAL

CONFIDENTIAL

VOLUME III
Vol 3

WAR DIARY

2nd BATTN. DUKE of WELLINGTON'S REGT

1st MARCH – 31st MARCH 1917.

3H
5 sheets

Original

WAR DIARY
or
INTELLIGENCE SUMMARY

(Erase heading not required.)

2/7 Duke of Wellington's Regt

Instructions regarding War Diaries and Intelligence Summaries are contained in F.S. Regs., Part II. and the Staff Manual respectively. Title Pages will be prepared in manuscript.

Place	Date	Hour	Summary of Events and Information	Remarks and references to Appendices
BEAUMONT-HAMEL	1/3/17		General Regt Routine. Batt HQ at Q.11.d.1.8. (Y RAVINE)	
"	2/3/17		" " " Working parties & Burying parties	
"	3/3/17		" " " 2/Lts TANNER & POPPY proceeded to Divisional Course	
"	4/3/17		Orders received for Battn to move to FORCEVILLE. Spent morning clearing out dug-outs. 500 men on working party at BEAUCOURT. Left Y RAVINE at 2.30 p.m. After heavy, muddy journey arriving FORCEVILLE about 4.30 p.m. Batt H.Q. P.21.d.0.5.	
FORCEVILLE	5/3/17		General Regt Routine. Received Divisional orders for an attack by 186th Bgde. HQ officers & O.C. coys were present at a practice of the above by 5th & 6th Battns D.o.W. in the afternoon. All available officers viewed the ground over which the practice was to practise the attack. On the afternoon (letters) A & B coys	
"	6/3/17		shot this attack. Major CHAMBERLIN Major & O.C. coys went to Forward Area [L.28.9.L34.] to reconnoitre. Weather still cold though much is prevalent.	under 2/Lt ORMEROD (T.O.)
"	7/3/17		Battn provided working parties. Runners sent from each coy to H.Q. to learn 9 H routes in Forward Area." (L.28.9.L34). Weather frosty. Snow	
"	8/3/17		Battn found working parties. on the ground, visit :- N. Easterly. Corps Commander Gen. FANSHAWE visited H.Q. of the Regt. G-in-C came thro' in afternoon	

Army Form C. 2118

WAR DIARY
or
INTELLIGENCE SUMMARY
(Erase heading not required.)

2/7 Duke of Wellington's Regt.

Instructions regarding War Diaries and Intelligence Summaries are contained in F.S. Regs., Part II. and the Staff Manual respectively. Title Pages will be prepared in manuscript.

Place	Date	Hour	Summary of Events and Information	Remarks and references to Appendices
FOUCAUCOURT	9/3/17		Wind N. Easterly, heavy fall of snow. Regt. Routine, majority of Regt. on working parties.	
"	10/3/17		Regt. Routine: working parties. 2/Lt Ormerod & party returned from reconnaissance in Forward Area.	Capt T.M. Rutherford, Capt E.H. Watson, Lt N.T. Lawton & 2/Lt Hawksfield evacuated to Hospital.
"	11/3/17	12.0 noon	Regt Routine. Sunday. Quiet day. 4.26.6.34	
"	12/3/17		Working Parties. Weather sunny & fine.	
"	13/3/17		" 2/Lt A. M'Alalieu appointed assistant Transport Officer.	
"	14/3/17	10.30 a.m.	Received orders to proceed to Bois d'Hollande to be in Brigade Reserve. Battalion left 2.30 p.m. and arrived at destination about 5.30 p.m. Battalion accommodated in dug-outs which were muddy & unsavoury. Working Parties found. Battalion in new quarters about midnight, the companies were ordered to report to 167th Inf. Bgde. (B&D. letter etc).	
BOIS d'HOLLANDE	15/3/17		Two companies left about 2.0 a.m. At 5.30 p.m. Battalion moved into line and took over from 2/4 K.O.Y.L.I. with a 300y frontage. B & D companies reformed in old new Battalion H.Q. A.B&C companies went into front line. O.D. Coy. in reserve. Lt. Col. W. Clifford D.S.O. proceeded on leave. Major F.G. Chamberlin assumed temporary command of Regiment.	

1875 Wt. W.593/826 1,000,000 4/15 J.B.C. & A. A.D.S.S./Forms/C.2118.

WAR DIARY
INTELLIGENCE SUMMARY

Army Form C. 2118

Place	Date	Hour	Summary of Events and Information	Remarks and references to Appendices
LINE (L2 & A)	16/3/17		Provisional orders for supporting 2/4 D of W in an attack received. We were to support by 3 strong patrols.	
"	17/3/17		Lt Lockwood assumed duty of Transport Officer. Lt H. Rowbotham evacuated to hospital. Received orders to send forward 3 officer patrols to junction of Resurrection Burgoy Trenches to tooth up the trenches running North, East & West. Lt Gleag & 2 Lts. Harris & Furniss detailed. 12.0 noon the whole line moved forward and took up a line along the road between Burguoy & Achiet-le-Petit. Company patrols failed to get in touch with the enemy. Major G.E. Kelly, K.R.C. assumed command of the battalion.	
"	18/3/17	10.0 a.m	Provisional orders for composition of advanced guard received. Received orders to withdraw all troops which orders were cancelled soon after. 2 in were ordered to proceed to square 8 2a. Men quartered in dug outs in Bihaucourt Trench & in shelters in Logeast Wood. It appears that we had been shelled out of front line.	57° N.W. MAR
VICINITY OF LOGEAST WOOD	19/3/17		Dug outs whittens. W.P.s provided. Remainder of battalion mended road near our quarters. Raining in afternoon.	
"	20/3/17		W.P.s for road repairs. Weather wet tho' sunny; 2/Lt G Clifford evacuated to hospital. 6.30 p.m:- Received orders to be ready tomorrow early next morning. Major G.P. Kelly K.R.C received orders to relinquish command of this unit & take over the 17th Middlesex Regt. Authority SG/4/62 dated 20/3/17. Major F.G. Chamberlin, M.C. under Corps authorisation assumed command.	

WAR DIARY
or
INTELLIGENCE SUMMARY

Army Form C. 2118

(Erase heading not required.)

Place	Date	Hour	Summary of Events and Information	Remarks and references to Appendices
Vicinity of LOQEAST WOOD	21/3/17		Major G. C. Kelly R.A.C. left about 12.0 noon. Battalion "standing to" Spent day in cleaning up. Major P.H. Rutherford reported to hospital at Bailleul.	
"	22/3/17		Still awaiting move orders. Capt T.M. Rutherford gassed. 2/Lt Street reported for duty	
"	23/3/17		W.P.s provided. Weather cold & frosty	
"	24/3/17		400 men on Railway working party at Pusieux. Arranged to move Battn HQ & "D" coy into LOGEAST WOOD.	
LOGEAST WOOD	25/3/17		BATTN providing W.P.s for railway. Moved over HQ into spacious dug-out in Logeast Wood which we named "HENHAM PLACE".	A 25.d.9.1 57°N.W.
"	26/3/17		Railway W.P. (400 men) Weather wet & miserable. Men in shelters with a few dug-outs. Major Chamberlin promoted Lt-Colonel.	
"	27/3/17		W.P.s Railway. Weather more pleasant.	
"	28/3/17		" Raining	
"	29/3/17		" 1 coy remained in camp to bathe & overhaul. P.H. Schmidt to G.A. Shaw reported from 6th Army School. Took charge of Batt. Lewis guns. 2/Lt N.T. Lawton.	
"	30/3/17		W.P.s Railway of 3 companies. 1 coy in camp on Gas & Platoon training. 2/Lt D. Haythorne reported from Gas Course.	
"	31/3/17		" 2/Lt F.L. Jones & 2/Lt Lincolnshire Regt reporting for duty as Coy & [illegible]	

ORIGINAL

1914

CONFIDENTIAL

WAR DIARY

2/7th Duke of Wellington's Regt.

Period:- 1st April 1917. to 30th April 1917.

VOLUME 4

4H
9 sheets

Army Form C. 2118

WAR DIARY
or
INTELLIGENCE SUMMARY
(Erase heading not required.)

2/7 Duke of Wellington's Regt

Instructions regarding War Diaries and Intelligence Summaries are contained in F.S. Regs., Part II. and the Staff Manual respectively. Title Pages will be prepared in manuscript.

Place	Date	Hour	Summary of Events and Information	Remarks and references to Appendices
HENHAM PLACE LOG EAST 1N/16D	1/4/17		Batt'n provided M.T's for railway construction to ACHIET-LE-GRAND. Orders received to move to ACHIET-le-GRANDE.	
"	2/4/17		C.O made arrangements with T.T.O at ACHIET-le-GRANDE for W.P's. 200 by night & similar number by day. Batt'n commenced to move at 3 p.m. New quarters in tents at YORK CAMP (51 D A 99.) 2nd Echelon W.P. joined us in new quarters. Advance storm started at about 4 p.m. 2/Lt E TANNER reported from Duel course & 2/Lt T R DOBBY reported to hospital.	R/map 57c N.W
YORK CAMP	3/4/17		Orders received to move to MORY to the in support to the 185th In Bgde. Lts. A.T. GLOAG & J. VAUGHAN sent to reconnoitre road. Wet & miserable day.	
"	4/4/17		Moved to MORY about 2:0 p.m. Billetted in broken down houses. Phillis made from local material. Took over from 2nd Batt. Royal Warwickshire Regt. Batt'n HQ in house near church (T32A 8.9.0)	
MORY	5/4/17		Batt'n provided W.P's on roads. Major P.E. COCKBURN M.C. reported from Yth Bunema resumed duties g Regt. 2nd in Command. 2/Lt T HAWKSFIELD reported from hospital + 2/Lt E D NAYE joined us reinforcement officer. About 5:20 p.m. a mine exploded at the x roads inflicting about 30 casualties chiefly on "A" Company. 2/Lt L. KERSHAW went to hospital from shell shock due to same.	
"	6/4/17		Batt'n providing W.P's on Roads. Weather sunny. Capt W.V.HAIGH went down the line for R.F.C interview.	
"	7/4/17		Wet & windy day finding W.P's on roads.	
"	8/4/17		Orders for attack on Bullecourt- issued & companies commenced special training for normal attack in open warfare.	
"	9/4/17		Miserable day snowing. Heel Front Brders to move forward received. Standers packed at HQ ready for notice to move.	
"	10/4/17		"Standing to" from 1 o'clock awaiting orders to move. Men cancelled standars for Railway Embank'. 155th In'Bgde. order & copy Instructions the line "O" and were forwarded to 2/Lt J CLIFFORD reported from hospital NW of L26ST-SW-MEIN	

WAR DIARY
or
INTELLIGENCE SUMMARY

2/7 Duke of Wellingtons Regt.

Army Form C. 2118

Place	Date	Hour	Summary of Events and Information	Remarks and references to Appendices
MORY	11/4/17		Received orders to move forward at 6 a.m. Moved along Mory-Ecoust road remaining in field by road until evening. If not in return of all arms were ordered to go forward. Anzac Div attacked on night, gained their objective but had to fall back on their original line. Battn returned to Mory about 6 p.m.	
"	12/4/17		Ordered to take over line from 2/6 West Yorks & part of 7/8 W.Y. Relief carried out by Major E.C.P. Cockburn M.C. Complete about 3.45 a.m. Capt Hough returned to took over his company.	
LINE	13/4/17		Holding line with 3 coys finding 6 posts & 1 company along Railway Cutting Embankment. Battn HQ at C.20.d.88. Took over a post from 4th Bn Australians 13th at U.28.c.9.4. Heavily shelled during morning but casualties were light. Railway Embankment & Battn HQ bombarded unhealthy. Lt J Vaughan fired Bangalore torpedoes. This party completely destroyed GBC posts. Provided carrying party of 80 men for moving 7500lb dumps.	Appendix + L
"	14/4/17		Patrol report by 2/4 H Haythorne attached.	
"	15/4/17		From down until 6.30 a.m enemy heavily shelled our position Afterwards learnt he had attacked on our right. Continued shelling during the whole of the morning. Intcr company relief:- "C" coy relieved "B" coy on our right sector. Relief complete about 11.30 p.m. "D" coy first forced to evacuate owing to heavy shelling. They westheren about 150 to support were afterwards re-established.	
"	16/4/17		Left company relieved by 2 coys of 2/5 K.O.Y.L.I. Complete about 3.15 a.m. W.P.s for entrenching parties in front of Ecoust unable to carry on owing to heavy shelling of our line. Remained relief of remainder of Battalion	

Army Form C. 2118

WAR DIARY
or
INTELLIGENCE SUMMARY 2/7 Duke of Wellington's R
(Erase heading not required.)

Instructions regarding War Diaries and Intelligence Summaries are contained in F.S. Regs, Part II. and the Staff Manual respectively. Title Pages will be prepared in manuscript.

Place	Date	Hour	Summary of Events and Information	Remarks and references to Appendices
LINE	17/4/17		Batt. relieved by 2nd Bn Queen's Regt. Comps letter about 11p.m. 2/Lt E.H.D WALKER wounded outside Batt. HQ during relief	
	18/4/17		2/Lts T.V.HOUGHTON, S. RHODES, T.I. BRIERLEY reported on reinforcement of Officers. Moved into French shelters S.E. of MORY. Batt. HQ near Church. Everyone tired, easy reveille. Batt. 56/for relieved up until midday. Camp then moved to B.21 d 5.4. Capt T.M RUTHERFORD & 2/Lt A HAYTHORNE evacuated to hospital	Capt T.M RUTHERFORD & 2/Lt
MORY	19/4/17		Batt. Routine. chiefly cleaning up.	
	20/4/17		Batt. moved into B.26.c.6.6. Fine sunny day. Lt G.A SHAW evacuated to hospital. Batt. training for the attack.	
	21/4/17		"A" Coy. attacked field in oval'n S. of Ecoust. Commenced 10pm Finished 1.30 a.m. Dull day. Regt Routine. Lt & Qm W.B GILES evacuated to hospital. R.S.M. G.A THOMSON appointed acting Q.M. R.S.M F OGDEN assumes duties of R.S.M.	
	22/4/17		Church parade. Companies practised attack	
	23/4/17	9 a.m.	Bgde practice in attack attended by Div Gen. Practise forming up on a tape line east of MORY - BEHAGNIES Track. Drotos attended	
	24/4/17		Practice with German grenades commenced under Lieut Vaughan	
	25/4/17		General regimental routine. Practice in the attack as a Battalion, by Companies and by Platoons.	
		9 p.m.	Practice in forming up on the tape line and moving forward with satisfactory results.	

Army Form C. 2118

WAR DIARY
or
INTELLIGENCE SUMMARY
(Erase heading not required.)

Instructions regarding War Diaries and Intelligence Summaries are contained in F.S. Regs, Part II. and the Staff Manual respectively. Title Pages will be prepared in manuscript.

Place	Date	Hour	Summary of Events and Information	Remarks and references to Appendices
MORY	28/4/17		General regimental routine. Lieut. J. QUARNBY reported as reinforcement and posted to "C" Coy. Fine day.	
	29/4/17		Fine spring day. Instruction given by an officer of R.E. in intensive digging and construction of strong points.	
	30/4/17		Fine day. Training continued in the construction of strong points.	
			H. Chamberlin Lieut Colonel, Commanding 2/4"Bn. Duke of Wellington's Regt.	
			2.5.17.	
			CONSOLIDATION ET OUST :-	
LINE	16/4/17		Supplement to entry of April 15/4/17. Act of gallantry on the part of Lt Stretchbearers of "B" Coy by name Gargale, Bradbury, Wray and Lockwood. They carried in to a.d.s. Sergeant Henry Shutfield Lt. GOLDSELLER of 2/5th Duke's Regt through the German wire having moved him from the enemy first line.	
	2.5.17.		H. Chamberlin Lt. Col. Comg 2/4th Duke of Wellington's Regt. 2.5.17.	

Army Form C. 2118

WAR DIARY
or
INTELLIGENCE SUMMARY
(Erase heading not required.)

2/7 Duke of Wellington's Regt

Place	Date	Hour	Summary of Events and Information	Remarks and references to Appendices
HEBUTERNE PLACE LOUVENCOURT	1/4/17		Batt'n forwarded W.P.s for railway construction. Orders received to move to ACHIET-LE-GRANDE	
"	2/4/17		C.O. made arrangements with R.T.O. at ACHIET-LE-GRANDE for W.Ps. 200 by night & similar number by day. Batt'n commenced to move at 3 p.m. New quarters in tents at YORK CAMP. (5.10 A.99) 200 men on W.P. joined us in new quarters. Started at about 4 p.m. 2/Lt E. TANNER reported from Duty course & 2/Lt T.R. POPPY reported sick in hospital. Snow storm	R/Map. 57 - N.W.
YORK CAMP	3/4/17		Orders received to move to MORY later in support with the 185th Inf. Bgde. Lts A.T. GLOAG & J. VAUGHAN sent to reconnoitre road. Wet & miserable day.	
"	4/4/17		Moved to MORY about 2 p.m. Billeted in broken down houses Billets made from unnatural. Took over from 2nd Batt. Royal Warwickshire Regt.	
MORY	5/4/17		Batt. HQ in house near church (B32 F.9.0) Batt. provided W.Ps on roads. Major F.E. COCKBURN M.C. rejoined from the Rangers & resumed duties of Regt 2nd in Command. 2/Lt T. HAWKSFIELD reported from hospital. 2/Lt E.P. KAYE joined as reinforcement officer. About 5:20 p.m. a mine exploded at the cross roads inflicting about 30 casualties chiefly on "A" Company. Batt. provided W.Ps on roads Weather sunny. (Capt. N.W. HAIGH went down the line for R.F.C. interview.)	
"	6/4/17		Wet & windy day - finding W.Ps on roads	
"	7/4/17		Orders for attack on "Bullecourt" issued. Companies commenced special training for mimic attack in open warfare	
"	8/4/17		Miserable day raining but brilliant sun - Orders received. Limbers packed at HQ ready for mimic return	
"	9/4/17		"Standing to" from 6 o'clock awaiting orders to move. Mimic cancelled about 7:15 a.m. 185 & 2/Bgde order: 1 coy to reinforce the line. "D" coy went forward to Railway embankment N.W. of VRAUCOURT. 2/Lt G CLIFFORD reported from hospital	
"	10/4/17			

Army Form C. 2118

Instructions regarding War Diaries and Intelligence Summaries are contained in F.S. Regs., Part II. and the Staff Manual respectively. Title Pages will be prepared in manuscript.

INTELLIGENCE SUMMARY
or
(Erase heading not required.)

2/7 Duke of Wellingtons. Reg't

Place	Date	Hour	Summary of Events and Information	Remarks and references to Appendices
~~Hipping~~ Mory	11/4/17		Received orders to move forward at 6 a.m. Moved along Mory-Ecoust road removing on field by road until evening. 9 officer column of all arms had been ordered to go forward. Anzac Div attacked on night, gained their objective but had fall back on their original line. Battln returned to Mory about 6 p.m.	
"	12/4/17		Ordered to take over line from 2/6 West Yorks & part of 2/8 W.Y. Relief carried out by Major E.C.F. Cockburn M.C. Complete about 3.45 a.m. Capt Haigh returned & took over his company.	
Line	13/4/17		Patrolling line with 3 coys finding Ghosts 41 company along Railway Cutting Embankment. Battln HQ at C.24.88. Took over a post from 46th Bns Fusiliers 13n at U.29.c.5.4. Heavily shelled during morning but casualties were light. Railway Embankment & Battln HQ particularly unhealthy. Lt J Vaughan MC died of wounds. Bangalore torpedoes arrived. This party of about 1-1½ coys employed by RE's to fill party for moving night. Riding Dumps.	Appendices 1 & 2
"	14/4/17		Patrol report by 2/4 D Haythornthwaite attached.	
"	15/4/17		From dawn until 8.30 a.m enemy heavily shelled our position. Afterwards learnt he had attacked on our right. Continued shelling during the whole of the morning. Inter-company relief: "C" coy relieved "B" coy on our right. Relief complete about 11.30 p.m. "D" coy first tried to evacuate owing to heavy shelling. They withdrew about 1100 & support were afterwards re-established.	
"	16/4/17		Left company relieved by 2 coys of 2/5 Royts. Comp. left about 3.15 a.m. W.Y.'s for entrenching parties in front of Ecoust, unable to carry out owing to heavy shelling of our line. Remained relief of remainder of Battalion	

WAR DIARY or INTELLIGENCE SUMMARY

Army Form C. 2118

2/7 Duke of WELLINGTON'S

Place	Date	Hour	Summary of Events and Information	Remarks and references to Appendices
LINE	17/4/17		Battn relieved by 2nd Bn Queen's Regt. Coys ctrd outside Batt HQ during relief. 2/Lt E.H.D WALKER wounded outside Batt HQ during relief. 2/Lts T.V HOUGHTON, S. RHODES, T.I BRIERLEY reported as rejoined rebel officers. Moved into French shelters S.E of Mory. Batn HQ near Church.	
"	18/4/17		Everyone tired, easy reveillé. Batt slept relaxed up until midday. Camp then moved to B.21. [erased] at 0.4. Capt T.M RUTHERFORD 9 2/Lt A HAYTHORNE evacuated to hospital.	
MORY	19/4/17	2	Batt Routine, chiefly cleaning up.	
"	20/4/17		Batt moved into B.2.b.6.6. Fine sunny day. Lt G.A SHAW evacuated to hospital. Batt training for the attack.	
"	21/4/17		"A" Day detailed itself in order to of Events. Commenced opn. Finished 1.30 a.m. Dull day. Regt Routine. Lt. & Qm HIS GREES evacuated to hospital R.S.M. S.A THOMSON appointed acting QM. R.S.M. F OGDEN assumes duties of R.S.M.	
"	22/4/17		Church parade. Companies practised attack	
"	23/4/17	9 a.m	Bgde practice in attack attended by Div. Gen. Practise forming up on a tape line East of MORY - BEHAGNIES Track. Bodies attached.	Appendices
"	24/4/17		Practise with German grenades commenced under Lieut Vaughan	
"	25/4/17		General regimental routine. Practise in the attack as a Battalion, by Companies and by Platoons	
"		9 pm	Practise in forming up on the tape line and moving forward — most satisfactory results.	

Army Form C. 2118

WAR DIARY
or
INTELLIGENCE SUMMARY

(Erase heading not required.)

Instructions regarding War Diaries and Intelligence Summaries are contained in F. S. Regs., Part II. and the Staff Manual respectively. Title Pages will be prepared in manuscript.

Place	Date	Hour	Summary of Events and Information	Remarks and references to Appendices
MORY	28/4/17		General regimental routine. 2/Lieut S. QUARMBY reported as reinforcement and posted to "C" Coy. Fine day.	
	29/4/17		Fine spring day. Instruction given by an officer of R.E. in intensive digging and construction of strong points.	
	30/4/17		Fine day. Training continued in the construction of strong points.	
			R.Chambers Lieut Colonel. Commanding 2/4th Bn Duke of Wellington's Regt.	
			2.5.17.	
			CONSOLIDATION. ET OUEST:- Supplement to entry of April 15th/917. Act of gallantry on the part of 4 Stretcherbearers of "B" Coy by name, Garside, Bradbury, Wray and Lockwood. They carried in to add Clinic under heavy shell fire at GOLDSELLER of 2/5th York Regt through the German wire having rescued him from the enemy first line.	
LINE	1/5/17			
			R.Chambers Lt Col Comg 2/4th Duke of Wellington's Regt. 2.5.17.	

2.5.17

appear that no serious damage has been caused to enemy wire by our artillery. It is reported that direct hits have failed to seriously break the wire, which is deep but not dense.

APPENDIX I WAR DIARY

6. PATROLS Our own. A patrol consisting of Lt. HAYTHORNE and 3 O.R. 2/7th.D. of W's.Regt. left the Post at U.27.d.2.4. at 9.15 p.m. They proceeded along the road towards BULLECOURT and found a large Mine Crater completely blocking the road at U.27.d.6.8. (approx) At U.27.d.5.9. two knife rests one behind the other. A diagonal gap about 2 feet wide was noticed in the first one. The Patrol was sniped at this point and then fired on by M.G. from U.27.b.6.1. (where trench meets road). Patrol then proceeded along outside of wire in N.W. direction for about 250 yards, when they were sniped from U.27.b.1.6. (where trench meets road) Patrol then retired to road (original line of advance) when heavy M.G. fire was opened on them from U.27.b.6.1. and U.28.a.2.1. Wire reported damaged but no actual gaps. Patrol returned at 10.45 p.m.

A patrol of 1 Officer and 3 O.R. left post at U.20.d.8.5. at the same time as above patrol and proceeded to cross roads at U.20.d.9.5. thence towards a point in enemy line at about U.21.a.7.1. This patrol corroborates the statements of the former patrol. Time of return 10.40 p.m.

CONFIDENTIAL

ORIGINAL Vol 5

WEST RIDING

2/7th. BN. DUKE OF WELLINGTON'S

WAR DIARY

FROM :- 1st. MAY 1917.

To :- 31st. MAY 1917.

VOLUME 5.

WAR DIARY or INTELLIGENCE SUMMARY

Army Form C. 2118

2/7 Duke of Wellington's

Place	Date	Hour	Summary of Events and Information	Remarks and references to Appendices
BEHAGNIES	1/5/17	—	General Regtl Routine. Notification received that this was X day. Operation Orders issued to all concerned. Orders of the day attached	B 26 c 6. 6 [10] APPENDIX I / II
	2/5/17		Batt. busy with necessary final preparations. Moved up to line at 11p.m. Zero hour 3.45 A.M. turned off from tapes line & battle for Bullecourt commenced.	
LINE	3/5/17	3.45	Reports received that part of Hindenburg line was occupied by our troops. Three posts were apparently installed & a number of posts were being carried on by sections. Report by 2/Lt F.G. Chamberlain attached. Casualties amongst officers were as follows. Killed – 2/Lt E.P. Kaye. Wounded: Major P.E. Cockburn M.C. 2/Lt T. Hawksfield, 2/Lt E. Tanner, Capt M.V. Haigh 2/Lt T.V. Haighton, Lt A.F. Gregg, 2/Lt J.I. Brierley, 3/Lt S. Rhodes, 2/Lt H. Furniss. Missing 2/Lt H.F. Street & 2/Lt E. Marlor. Casualties amongst O.Rs were about 200.	APPENDIX III
BEHAGNIES	4/5/17		Battalion relieved and returned to Behagnies. Batt. resting & cleaning up. Received orders to move into line again & take over from 2/6 D.O.W.	140
LINE	5/5/17		Relief complete about 3 a.m. Established 4 posts in forward line supported by 2 support posts. The whole under command of 2/Lt I. Maden. The remainder of the battalion along line of entrenchment fulling in with 2/6 & 2/5 D.O.W. The 2/6 D.O.W. were on our right & the 167 Bde on the left. Several wounded men brought in during the night.	Front Posts [140] Support Post [140]
	6/5/17		Quiet day, usual shelling. Casualties: light. Relieved at night by the 2/4 D.O.W. Battalion marched back to Behagnies.	140
MORY (C 31 C 5/8)	7/5/17		Battalion resting. Relieving up over Strays 2/5 West Yorks. Moved up to Ervillers at 8 p.m. Regt men in huts & further down lines	140

WAR DIARY or INTELLIGENCE SUMMARY

Army Form C. 2118

2/7 Duke of Wellington's Regt

Place	Date	Hour	Summary of Events and Information	Remarks and references to Appendices
ERVILLERS	8/5/17		GENERAL Regtn Routine. Reorganisation commenced. Miserable day with rain.	140
"	9/5/17		General Routine. Fair weather. Ordinary training carried out.	140
"	10/5/17		Fine day. "A" and "B" Coys under Capt G W Miller proceeded to MORY COPSE and were under orders of 2/10th Duke of Wellington's Regt from 11.0 a.m. to 5 p.m, during which hours the 2/10 Bn were under Readiness A to re-inforce the line.	140
"	11/5/17		Capt. E N Watson appointed second in command.	
"	12/5/17		Fine day. Ordinary training and Regtl routine carried out.	140
"	13/5/17		Fine day. Training as usual until noon. 2/Lt A HAYTHORNE reported back from hospital. 2/Lt. B. C. JOHNSON reported from 3rd Infantry Base Depot for duty. Relieved a company of 165th T.B.W. on the line. The whole batln went in to Sunken Rd Unzie & on attack was made on the Crucifix, Bullecourt (APPENDIX IV)	140
LINE	13/5/17		Heavily shelled away the whole of the day. 2/Lt T.S. Johnson killed & 2/Lt A HAYTHORNE wounded. Casualties fairly heavy. Major England 2/6 DofW. who was in charge of forward Positions relieved by Commanding Officer (Col F.G. Chew 2/Bn 19(?) DofW)	118
"	14/5/17		Posts Garrison of Sunken Rd. Still being heavily shelled. Our forward relieved by 2/5 D.Q.W. were found the front & support posts. Men tired out. Spent some time & cleaning up their rifles & making	140
"	15/5/17		fire step along embankment.	140
"	16/5/17		Enemy artillery extraordinarily quiet from "S" and "6" until noon. Enemy reported to have retired but our patrols found the Hindenburg Line occupied.	140
"	17/5/17		Touch was held with 56th Div who had relieved the 7th Div on our right. Thg were served with 2118 Attempts still being made to get forward	140

WAR DIARY or INTELLIGENCE SUMMARY

2/7 Duke of Wellingtons

Army Form C. 2118

Place	Date	Hour	Summary of Events and Information	Remarks and references to Appendices
LINE	18/5/17		During the whole day both side artillery was very quiet. Visited by Gen'l F.Boyd. 2/4 Hayward joined for duty. Relieved 7th 2/5 D/g/W in forward posts. Lt Vaughan took charge of the garrison. Capt Watson & Lt Lockwood & 2/4 1. Maden evacuated Hospital	110
"	19/5/17		Quiet day. 2/4 Hayward relieved Lt Vaughan in Sunken Rd.	110
"	20/5/17		Batln relieved by 2/5 York & Lancs complete about 12.30 a.m.	110
COURCELLES	21/5/17		Moved back to Courcelles. Billetted in tents Rest Supr all day. Spent the evening in cleaning up.	110
"	22/5/17		2 Companies had baths. Lts C.W.Lockwood & G.A.Snow returned from Hospital	110
"	23/5/17		Glorious day. General Rest Routine including firing on Range.	120
"	24/5/17		General Rest Routine	120
"	25/5/17		"	120
"	26/5/17		"	120
"	27/5/17		"	120
"	28/5/17		" 8 Officers from West Yorks attached for duty whilst we were awaiting Reinforcements.	120
"	29/5/17		Men a from camp to camp vacated by 22nd Manchester Regt ad Achiet-Le-Petit. Men accommodated in improvised shelters & tents. Camp rather	(L18 & 2.B)
ACHIET-LE-PETIT	30/5/17		2/Lt. Pearson, Gould, Cartwright, Spafforn & Hattersley reported for duty General Rest Routine	110
"	31/5/17		Lt Alexander (att from W.Y.) evacuated sick (accident)	110

B. Chambertain, Lt Col.
3.6.17 Comdg 2/7 Duke of Wellington Regt (West Riding)
In the Field.

APPENDIX I

SECRET.   COPY NO. 15

OPERATION ORDERS FOR ATTACK ON A SECTION OF THE
HINDENBURG LINE.

LT. COL. F.G. CHAMBERLIN, M.C., O. de C. COMMANDING
2/7th. BN. DUKE OF WELLINGTON'S REGT.   1st. MAY 1917.
....

Ref. Maps. EQUIST-ST-EIN, Edn. 3. 1. 10,000 and 57 C.H.W. 1. 20,000.

(1) The 186th. Infantry Brigade will attack and capture a section
of the HINDENBURG LINE on May 3rd.   Zero hour 3.30 a.m.
The first objective will be the trenches in U.20.b. and C.21.
The second objective will be the line of roadway from
U.22.b.5.5. to U.16.c.4.3. The third objective will be
HENDECOURT and a line running from U.12.c.7.7. - U.11.b.8.0 -
U.9.d.3.4. The attack will be carried out simultaneously
by the 185th. Infantry Brigade on the right, the 186th.
Infantry Brigade in the centre, and the 187th. Infantry
Brigade on the left. The right boundary for the 186th.
Infantry Brigade will be a line from U.27.a.6.7. to
Cross roads U.27.b.15.80., thence roadway to U.21.d.3.6.
From here the responsibility for the 186th. Infantry Brigade
extends to roadway U.22.d.0.3. - U.22.b.8.5., from thence a
line running East of HENDECOURT and THE CHATEAU in U.12.c.

(2) The boundary line between the 2/7th. Bn. Duke of Wellington's
Regt. and the 2/4th. Bn. Duke of Wellington's Regt. is
U.21.b.15.05 to trench junction at U.22.a.65.95, junction of
trench with roadway at U.17.a.80.38, road junction U.17.a.45.90
to road junction U.11.b.2.3., all inclusive to this
Battalion. Right boundary of the Battalion is from
U.21.d.0.7. to U.21.b.8.5., thence a line running East of
HENDECOURT and THE CHATEAU in U.12.c. The centre of the
Battalion will rest on the roadway from U.21.d.3.6. to
U.21.a.25.50 and thence to U.17.a.5.3. to U.12.a.0.3.

(3) OBJECTIVES.   2/7th. Bn. Duke of Wellington's Regt. is
responsible for the capture of the second and third
objectives.
'C' and 'A' Coys will form the leading wave in two lines.
'D' and 'B' Coys will form the second wave with 'B' and 'D'
Coys on the right respectively.
The leading wave will be responsible for the second objective.
As soon as this has been captured, 'D' and 'B' Coys will
leap frog over 'C' and 'A' Coys and form up in front of it
ready to push on and capture the third objective. The
forming up will be protected by barrage of 35 minutes, when
these 2 Coys will keep as close up to it as they can.
As soon as the second objective has been taken, it will be
consolidated and taken over by O.C. 2/5th. West Yorks Regt.
When that is cleared, 'C' and 'A' Coys will follow on to
support 'D' and 'B' Coys in capture and consolidation of the
third objective.

(4) FORMING UP.   At zero hour, minus ½ an hour, the Battalion
will be formed up ready to advance in two waves, with 4 lines
on a taped line from U.26.d.85.50 to U.26.c.0.3., the left
flank of 'A' Coy resting on the right flank of the 2/4th.
Bn. Duke of Wellington's Regt. Taped line is for leading
waves only. Battalion Headquarters in Embankment at U.26.c.

(5) REPORT CENTRE.   First, the battle position will be located
at the embankment in U.26.c. until the second objective has
been taken and the second barrage starts, when the Report
Centre will move up to about U.22.b.0.5. (boundary).

1.   F.F.O.

(6) **PARTIES.** O.C. 'A' Coy will detail 1 Party of 25 O.R. under 2/Lieut. J. Uhden, to report to Captain Bruce at the Advanced Brigade Dump at the Embankment.
O.C. 'B' Coy. will detail 1 party of 2 N.C.O's and 20 O.R. as a Carrying Party for the 213th. M.G. Coy. (A guide will be sent to conduct this party). Also 2 N.C.O's and 20 O.R. for the L.T.M.B.

(7) **PATROLS.** O.C. 'C' Coy will throw out 3 Patrols of 1 reliable N.C.O. and 10 men to proceed up 3 roads in square U.22 to clear this of the enemy before the main body proceeds

(8) **STRONG POINTS.** As soon as the first objective has been taken, Strong Points will be formed at :-

 (1) U.17.a.8.0.)
 (2) U.17.b.80.15.) 'C'
 (3) U.17.b.3.5.) Coy.
 (4) U.17.b.3.9.)

 (5) U.11.d.8.1.)
 (6) U.12.c.4.2.) 'D'
 (7) U.12.c.3.5.) Coy.
 (8) U.11.d.6.5.)

 (9) U.11.d.4.6.) 'B'
 (10) U.11.b.1.2.) Coy.

These two latter to be handed over to 2/4th. Bn. Duke of Wellington's Regt. as soon as possible after construction. 'A' Coy will garrison these until the relief.

(9) **FLANK BRIGADES.** Right Brigade will move 3 minutes in advance and the Left Brigade 2 minutes in advance of the 186th. Infantry Brigade.

(10) **PERSONNEL LEFT BEHIND.** The following personnel will not take part in the Operations :-
Capt. E.R.Watson.
Capt. T.M.Rutherford.
Capt. H.W.Knocker.
Lieut. G.A.Shaw.
2/Lt. J.S.Clapham.
2/Lt. C.Clifford.
2/Lt. E.G.Harris.
2/Lt. J.R.Quarmby.
2/Lt. A.Haythorne.
2/Lt. A.McMullen.
2/Lt. T.R.Pepny.
2/Lt. L.Marshaw.
CSM Flatt.
CSM Hill.
2 Signallers per Coy.
Gas Instructor (Cpl Gillard).
Bombing Instructor (2nd Warren).
2 Lewis Gun N.C.O's.
1 Cpl & 1 L/Cpl per Coy.
4 Snipers to be detailed by 2/Lt. H.Ormerod.
2 Rifle Grenadiers per Coy.
Orderly Room staff.
4 Lewis Gun Teams will remain in reserve at H.Qs. (1 per Coy)
Officers, N.C.O's and men detailed for Courses, who may answer for any of the above.

(11) **FLANK DIRECTION.** O.C. Coys will detail 1 Officer or good N.C.O. with Compass as guide for direction on flank.

(12) **OFFICER IN CHARGE OF THIRD OBJECTIVE.** Major G.L.C.Cockburn, M.C. will be in charge of the consolidation of the third objective. He will not go forward until report has been received that third objective has been captured and in course of consolidation, when he will take full control of Sector of the 2/7th. Bn. Duke of Wellington's Regt.

(13) **LIAISON OFFICER.** The Adjutant will proceed with 4 Runners to H.Q. of 51st. Bn. Australians.

(14) **FORWARD HEADQUARTERS.** Lieut.J.W.Charlesworth will reconnoitre the Forward Headquarters when second barrage starts.

N O T E S.

(1) Every Officer in the leading Companies will carry a Very Pistol – 2 men will be specially detailed to accompany each of these Officers and will carry 12 green 1" lights each.

(2) **Dress and Equipment.** In addition to his ordinary equipment, every Infantry Soldier will carry :-
 (a) 170 rounds S.A.A. (Carrying Parties, Bombers, Lewis Gunners, Runners and Signallers will carry 50 rounds S.A.A. only).
 (b) 2 Mills Grenades in the pockets for all troops.
 (c) 2 Sandbags.
 (d) 1 Flare.

All men of Bombing sections will carry 2 "P" Bombs for dealing with Dugouts.
Bombers will carry 8 Mills Grenades each in buckets.
Rifle Grenadiers will carry 8 Rifle Grenades each in buckets.
Picks and Shovels will be carried by the rear line of each wave.
All available Wire Cutters and Wire Breakers will be carried by selected men to deal with any wire remaining uncut. Tiversboles will be worn and waterproof sheets carried. All other kit to be packed in men's Wallets.
All troops will wear a piece of bright tin 4" square on the haversack.
Code words will not be used after Zero hour.
Watches will be synchronised at 12.30 p.m. and 5.30 p.m. on Y day.
Contact Aeroplanes will operate with the Infantry.
The urgent need for frequent Situation Reports is to be impressed on all concerned.
The S.O.S. Signal from Z day will be green lights or rockets.

/sgd/ F.L.JONES, Lieut. & Adjt.,
2/7th. Bn. Duke of Wellington's Regt.

62ND DIVISION.
ORDER OF THE DAY.

As the Division will shortly be going into action to take part in its first great battle, the Divisional Commander desires to assure all ranks of his complete confidence in their ability to defeat the German troops opposed to them.

That the 62nd (West Riding) Division will maintain its reputation for staunchness and grit - qualities for which Yorkshiremen have ever been famed - that they will gain all objectives and hold them against the most determined counter-attacks, is the firm conviction of the General Officer who is proud to be their Commander.

Major General.
Commanding 62nd (West Riding) Division.

May 1st 1917.

Appendix III

2/7th. BN. DUKE OF WELLINGTON'S REGT.

REPORT ON ATTACK MADE ON 3rd. MAY 1917.

Reference Maps, ECOUST-ST-MIEN 3. 1/10,000 and 57 C.N.W. 1/20,000

1. At 3.37 a.m. the 2/7th. Bn. Duke of Wellington's Regt. advanced to capture and consolidate objective line of roadway from U.22.b.8.5. - U.16.c.4.5. and village of HENDECOURT and a line running from U.12.c.7.7. - U.11.b.8.0. - U.9.d.2.4.
   Strength of Regt :- 14 Officers, 430 Other Ranks.
   Distribution :- In two waves, with 'C' Coy on the right and 'A' Coy on the left of the first wave, followed by 'D' Coy on the right and 'B' Coy on the left of the second wave.

2. In spite of the left Brigade losing direction and coming half right across its front, the Regiment continued its advance intact and successfully reached the sector of THE HINDENBURG LINE, U.21.d.3.5. - U.21.d.75.70., where it was met by a heavy Rifle and Machine Gun fire, both enfilade and direct, heavy casualties resulting owing to the barrage having fallen short of the trench, apparently leaving the enemy in force, and the wire only demolished in parts. In spite of this, the trench was entered by the Regiment and certain casualties to the enemy inflicted. From this point the attack became disorganised owing to Officer casualties. A number of men from 2/8th. West Yorks Regt and the 2/5th. Duke of Wellington's Regt joined forces with the 2/7th. Duke of Wellington's Regt at this stage. As above stated, the German Line was entered but owing to the disorganised condition of the troops and the enemy not having been in the least broken, the troops fell back on a line of shell holes and from there maintained their advance, being heavily shelled by all calibres, including fire shells, which in some instances were seen to burn the wounded, eventually posts being established at points U.21.d.1.3. - U.21.c.6.8. - U.21.c.7.5. - U.21.c.1.3. One party of the 2/7th. Bn. Duke of Wellington's Regt succeeded in pushing on through the 1st and 2nd line of enemy trench with some of the 2/8th. West Yorks Regt under one of the 2/7th. Bn. Duke of Wellington's Regt. Officers to U.22.b.3.7. (neighbourhood THE FACTORY). This was confirmed by aeroplane, but no report has been received from this party nor have any of them returned. It is surmised one of the three Officers missing was with this party.

3. Two reports sent in from Major Cockburn (who was sent out to clear up the situation), one in the morning and one late in the afternoon, very briefly stating what had taken place but owing to being wounded, stating nothing in detail immediately bearing on the situation. Otherwise no information available except what was obvious, that owing to the failure of right and left Brigades, both flanks apparently in the air.

4. Orders issued by the Officer Commanding, under the direction of the G.O.C. 186th. Infantry Brigade, to the nearest known post of the 2/7th. Bn. Duke of Wellington's Regt. in SUNKEN ROAD under Major Cockburn (U.20.d.8.2.) to whence he had retired, to retire to Railway Embankment U.26.c.5.0. so soon as it was dark, with as many men as he could collect.

5. This was carried into effect at 9.30 p.m. It was then found that nine out of the Officers who led off in the attack were casualties, three were missing, two only returning unhurt. Casualties in Other Ranks 2/3rds. of the strength in the advance.

    The 2/7th. Bn. Duke of Wellington's Regt. undoubtedly maintained its line of advance, even though crossed by other troops, until the enemy line was reached and "doggedly" carried out its task from 3.37 a.m. till dark, 9.30 p.m., when the Officers and Other Ranks remaining fell back on the Support Line as ordered.

Appendix IV

ORDERS for ATTACK by 2/7th. Bn. Duke of Wellington's
(W.R.) Regiment.

13.5.17.

Ref. Map :- ECOUST-ST-MEIN 1/10,000.

Minor operations to be carried out by 2/7th. Bn. Duke of Wellington's Regt. on night 13/14th. May to capture and consolidate line U.27.b.10.65 - U.20.d.25.20 including Crucifix mound.

The attack will be pushed with the greatest determination and will be carried out by 1 platoon under LIEUT. J.E. BEAUMONT on the left of the SUNKEN ROAD, U.21.c. and 1 platoon under LIEUT. J. VAUGHAN on the right of this road (U.21.c.5.9 - CRUCIFIX).

A party of 15 Other Ranks under Acting Company Sergeant Major Woolliscroft J. will proceed down this sunken road preceded by bombing section.

1 Lewis Gun and covering party will be detailed to protect the left flank at U.21.c.7.4, and 1 Lewis Gun on right flank at U.27.b.1.6.

The garrison of 50 Other Ranks will be left in Sunken Road from U.20.d.9.4. - U.21.c.5.0. under Capt.R.M.Watson. 2/Lieut. B.C. Johnson is attached to Capt. Watson for duty.

Capt. G.J.M. Miller will be in charge of operations.

The sunken road from U.21.c.5.0 forward will be the guide for direction.

O.C. Left Platoon will form a block at U.21.d.2.5. and O.C. Right Platoon will form one at U.27.b.1.7.

2 Stokes Mortars and 3 Machine Guns will assist in the operations.

    Dress :- Fighting Order.
              170 rounds S.A.A.
              2 Mills Bombs.
              2 'P' Bombs.

Zero hour 3.30 a.m.

Line of resistance - Sunken Road.

/Sgd/ H. ORMEROD, 2/Lieut. & Asst.Adjt.,
2/7th. Bn. Duke of Wellington's Regiment.

CONFIDENTIAL WAR DIARY

- of -

2/7th Bn. DUKE OF WELLINGTON'S REGIMENT.

From:- 1. 6. 1917.
To:- 30. 6. 1917.

WAR DIARY
or
INTELLIGENCE SUMMARY

(Erase heading not required.) 2/4th Bn. DUKE of WELLINGTON'S REGT.

Army Form C. 2118

Place	Date	Hour	Summary of Events and Information	Remarks and references to Appendices
ACHIET LE PETIT.	1/6/17		Regimental Routine. Fine day. Draft of 36 men received from 34th Inf. Base Depot.	10/L.12.C.S.2.
"	2/6/17		Regimental Routine.	
"	3/6/17		do.	
"	4/6/17		do. Draft of 32 men received from 34th I.B.D. Capt G.W. Miller appointed Second in Command. Lieut J. Vaughan posted to "B" Coy as Company Commander. Working party of 200 men detailed for work on 6/6/17 and 8/6/17.	
"	5/6/17		Regimental Routine.	
"	6/6/17		do. 2/Lieut W.A. Hinchcliffe reported for duty and posted to "C" Coy. (Authority :- 186th I.B. S/3214).	
"	7/6/17		2/Lieut Boxall left to rejoin his own Unit. 2/Lieut A. Pearson appointed assistant Intelligence and Sniping Officer. 2/Lieut G.A. Cartwright appointed assistant Bombing Officer.	
"	8/6/17		Working Parties.	
"	9/6/17		Regimental Routine. Fine day.	
"	10/6/17		Church Parade and Working Parties. Battalion Specialists now well on the way towards being trained, the men who had been taken to replace casualties doing exceedingly well.	
"	11/6/17		Regimental Routine.	

WAR DIARY
or
INTELLIGENCE SUMMARY

(Erase heading not required.) 1/4th Bn DUKE of WELLINGTON'S REGT.

Army Form C. 2118

Place	Date	Hour	Summary of Events and Information	Remarks and references to Appendices
ACHIET LE PETIT	11/6/19		5 men received from 34th I.B.D.	HQ
"	12/6/19	9.0 - 2.0pm	Brigade Practice attack. Not a huge success. Practice turnout at night.	HQ
"	"	2.0pm	Regimental Routine & Bathing.	HQ
"	13/6/19		Special training in Gas Drill. Regimental Routine	
"	14/6/19		2/Lieut. G.C. Stott reported for duty and posted to "C" Coy.	
"	"		Practice in march discipline. Regimental Routine.	
"	"		2/Lieut. W.A. Hinchcliffe transferred from "C" Coy to "D" Coy.	
"	"		2/Lieut B.G. Harris appointed Lewis Gun Officer and Bombing Officer.	
"	"		Special instruction in the Lewis gun.	
"	"		Cpl Ireland a.B. appointed Cook Sergeant.	HQ
"	"		Inoculation commenced.	HQ
"	"		2/Lieut G. Clifford posted to "D" Coy	HQ
"	15/6/19		Regimental Routine.	HQ
"	"		5 men received from 34th I.B.D.	HQ
"	16/6/19		Regimental Routine	HQ
"	17/6/17		New teams of Lewis Gunners practised on the Range. Good Results obtained	HQ
"	18/6/17		Snipers on Range.	HQ
"	19/6/17		Regimental Routine. Insufficient day Inoculation proceeding.	HQ
"	20/6/17		Three men taken on Strength from 34th I.B.D. Regimental Routine.	HQ
"	21/6/17		Regimental Routine.	HQ

WAR DIARY
or
INTELLIGENCE SUMMARY

(Erase heading not required.) 2/7 DUKE OF WELLINGTON'S REGT.

Army Form C. 2118

Place	Date	Hour	Summary of Events and Information	Remarks and references to Appendices
ACHIET LE PETIT	22/6/17		Lt. T.H Chambers, 2nd Lt. F. Muff, 2nd Lt. H. Thornton and 14 other ranks – thirteen of which were casuals – reported for duty from 3rd I.B.D. Three Companies off duty/Innoculation.	H.P.
"	23/6/17		2/Lieut. J.E Davies, 5th Welsh Regt reported for duty. Regimental Routine.	H.O
"	24/6/17		Brigade Church parade in the morning. Battalion resting afternoon.	H.O
"	25/6/17		Regimental Routine.	H.O
"		3.45p.m	2/Lieut S. Harris and 4 other ranks in a premature bomb explosion in grenade training trench. 2 other ranks killed, 2/Lt S. Harris and 5 other ranks wounded.	H.O L.1.2.c.5.2.
"	26/6/17		2/Lieut R.G. Harris died of wounds. Received orders to move to FAVREUIL area. Paraded in camp at 3.p.m and arrived there about 6.15 p.m. Bad camp. Dull day.	H.O
"A" Camp L.13.c.5.5.	27/6/17		Usual inspections carried out. Company Commanders went up the line in the afternoon to take over. Battalion proceeded to relieve NOREUIL Sector at 10.5 p.m. Easy journey up. 2/Lieut J.A. Cartwright assumed duties of Intelligence Officer, Bombing Officer and Lewis Gun Officer.	H.O
LINE	28/6/17		Line held by the Battalion and 2 Companies of the 2/6th Bn. Duke of Wellington's Regt. 185th Infantry Brigade on the right and	H.O

WAR DIARY
or
INTELLIGENCE SUMMARY

(Erase heading not required.) 2/4th Duke of Wellington's Regt.

Army Form C. 2118

Place	Date	Hour	Summary of Events and Information	Remarks and references to Appendices
LINE	28/6/17		2/5th Duke of Wellington's Regt on the left. Line extended from C.11.d.4.4 to U.29.d.5.4. 2/4th Duke of Wellington's Regt constituted the front line. A broken trench held by 2/5th Duke of Wt. Regt ("C" and "D" Coys). The left portion Battalion Headquarters at C.5.d.4.7. firstly in shelters and then in dugouts. Miserable weather. Plenty of work to be done in improving sector. On the whole very quiet. Major S. R. MASON. M.C. 6th York & Lancs Regt. joined for duty as Second in command. Casualties - Nil.	O.31.U.24. MO.
"	29/6/17		Day very quiet and wet.	MO
"	30/6/17		Wet day. Usual line routine, men still busy improving line.	MO

J. Omerod 2/Lt
for Lieut Colonel
2/4th Duke of Wellington's
Eng Regt

2/4th Duke of Wellington's Regt.

SECRET WAR DIARY
- of -

2/7th Bn. DUKE OF WELLINGTON'S REGIMENT.

From:- 1st July 1917

To:- 31st July 1917.

Rendered in accordance with F.S. Regs.

Volume VII

WAR DIARY or INTELLIGENCE SUMMARY

Army Form C. 2118

2/7 Duke of Wellington's Regt.

Place	Date	Hour	Summary of Events and Information	Remarks and references to Appendices
LINE	1.7.17		Fine. On the whole quiet. Normal Line Routine. Wiring A Co's Sector from C5 & B6. 10 O.R. shelled with 150 mms. on Patrol Rd. Glory T20 O.R. as covering party for R.E.'s. No enemy encountered & no casualties.	
	2.7.17		Fine. Quiet. Normal line routine. Continued Wiring Trench. A Patrol 2 Lt. J.Q. Barraclough + 30 O.R. out to reconnoitre Mines & craters. There were no casualties.	
	3.7.17		Fine. Battalion had skilled Trench improvements carried on from Hobart Avenue. Patrol 2 Lt. G. Kattersley + 4 O.R. to ruin trench with Brigade on right etc.	
	4.7.17		2 Casualties	
			Fine & Quiet. Battalion busy improving line. Patrol 2 Lt. T. Squarmby & 6 good R.B.'s 12 OR Casualties	
	5.7.17		Fine. Quiet. Trench improvements during the day. Battalion relieved commenced at 11.45 pm & completed 2.0 am 6/7/17. Relieving battalion 2/4 K.O.Y.L.I. Relief in good order. No casualties. Companies proceeded independently to 'A' camp (I.13.c.5.5).	
"A" Camp I.13.c.5.5.	6/7/17		Fine. Interior Economy	
	7/7/17		Fine. Training Commenced	
	8/7/17		Very Wet. All parades cancelled.	

Army Form C. 2118

WAR DIARY
or
INTELLIGENCE SUMMARY
(Erase heading not required.)

2/7 Duke of Wellington's R/

Instructions regarding War Diaries and Intelligence Summaries are contained in F.S. Regs., Part II. and the Staff Manual respectively. Title Pages will be prepared in manuscript.

Place	Date	Hour	Summary of Events and Information	Remarks and references to Appendices
A Camp I.13.b.55	9.7.17		Heavy rain all day. Instruction carried on in tents by Platoons. Rifles and equipment cleaned.	
–do–	10.7.17		Showery – Two Companies bathed. Battalion engaged Training	
–do–	11.7.17		Fine. Two Companies bathed. One Company worked on construction of A Range. One Company practised Ranging. M.C. awarded to 2nd Lieut H. FURNISS and 2/Lieut E TANNER. (Divisional R.O. 685)	appendix
–do–	12.7.17		Fine. Training.	
–do–	13.7.17		Fine. Working party of one Company engaged on construction of A Range. In morning. Battalion moved to O.30.a.55 to relieve the 2/5th West Yorks Rgt. in support on the 9.30 pm. LAGNICOURT Sector. No Casualties. 2nd Suffolks in support on our right.	
LINE	14.7.17		Fine. Working parties employed under R.E. Supervision digging dugouts and carrying materials. 250 men employed daily. Casualties Nil	
–do–	15.7.17		Fine. Working parties supplied as previous day. Casualties Nil.	
–do–	16.7.17		–do– –do– Casualties Nil	
–do–	17.7.17		Very heavy showers. Working parties supplied as previous day. Casualties Nil. 2/Lieuts J.S. CLAPHAM, J. BUCKLEY and H.L. HOPPER reported for duty and were posted to A, D & C Companies respectively.	

WAR DIARY or INTELLIGENCE SUMMARY

Army Form C. 2118

(Erase heading not required.)

7/n Duke of Wellington Rgt

Place	Date	Hour	Summary of Events and Information	Remarks and references to Appendices
LINE	18.7.17		Line. Working Parties as on previous day. 2/Lieut A. PEARSON was sent down the line with trench fever.	Appx A
–do–	19.7.17		Line. Working Parties as on previous day. 2/Lt G. CARTWRIGHT reported for duty on return from Lewis Gun Course.	Appx A
–do–	20.7.17		Line. Working Parties as on previous day. 2/Lieut J. B. CLAPHAM was detailed as Agricultural Officer to report at VAUX. 2/Lieut DAVIES attached to report to 457 Field Coy R.E.	Appx A
–do–	21.7.17		The Battalion relieved the 2/6th DUKE OF WELLINGTONS REGIMENT in sect. of Brigade Sector. Relief completed without casualties at 12.10 a.m. Battalion Boundary C.18.6.54 to C.12.a.54. Battn HQ at C.17.d.71. 185th Infantry Brigade on left and 2/4th DUKE OF WELLINGTONS REGT on right. A Coy in forward posts B.9, B.10, B.11, B.12. and B Company in posts B.13, B.14, B.15 & B.16. C & D Companies in the Main Line of Resistance C supporting A and A supporting B. Sector in great need of improvement. A covering patrol of 2nd Lieut F. MUFF and 12 O/R. No enemy seen and no casualties.	Appx A
–do–	22.7.17		Line. Work commenced cleaning posts, Trenches & S.A.A. Bomb dumps making good deficiencies. Enemy Artillery a little more active. Two patrols out – Captain ALEXANDER, 2nd Lieut BUCKLEY and 21 O/R. from 10.45 P.M. till 2 A.M. and 2nd Lieut F. MUFF and 11 O/R from 1 a.m. 5 3 a.m. Object of both Patrols to obtain identity of no mans land. No casualties to	Appx A

WAR DIARY or INTELLIGENCE SUMMARY

Army Form C. 2118

Place	Date	Hour	Summary of Events and Information	Remarks and references to Appendices
LINE	23/7/17		Fine. Trenches improved throughout. Wiring done in front of M.L.R. Two Patrols out - Captain ALEXANDER and 12 O/R from 1.10 A.M. to 3.00 A.M., and 2/Lt C.G. STOTT and 11 O/R from 11 P.M. to 1 A.M. Object reconnoitring No Man's Land. No casualties.	W.D.
—do—	24/7/17		Fine. Quiet. 63 yards of trenches made ready for duck boarding and 120 yards deepened and widened. Wiring carried on in front of M.L.R. posts. Fighting Patrol 2nd Lieut F. MUFFY, 2nd Lieut J. BUCKLEY and 83 O/R left at 10.30 P.M. returning at 3 A.M. Object to reconnoitre enemy positions. A post was discovered at C.12 & 9.2 and during work 2 other posts were brought back by Patrol, post having been demolished. One casualty - Sergeant Allen, bayonet wound. Congratulatory message. See appendix. Another Patrol of 2/Lieut Huncliff and 10 O/R was out from 1 A.M. to 3.30 A.M. Object to make preparatory reconnaissance of CRATER at D7 C 6.4. No casualties.	Appendix
—do—	25/7/17		Showery. Quiet. Work was carried on deepening & widening trenches. 33 yards being made ready for duckboards. C & D Companies relieved A & B Companies respectively. Relief completed at 1.10 A.M. without casualties. Patrol as covering party for relief 2/Lieut HATTERSLEY and 10 O/R out from 10.30 to 1.30 A.M.	W.D.

WAR DIARY
or
INTELLIGENCE SUMMARY
(Erase heading not required.)

Army Form C. 2118

1/7 Duke of Wellington's Rgt

Place	Date	Hour	Summary of Events and Information	Remarks and references to Appendices
LINE	26/7/17		Work continued on trenches. Fine. Quiet. LIEUT. W.C. POGSON reported from the 3/4th 1 B.D. for duty. Wiring in front of M.L.R. continued and firstbelt completed. Patrol of Captain ALEXANDER T & Lieut T BUCKLEY were out from 11 pm to 1 am - Object reconnaissance - No enemy encountered - No casualties.	MWS
-do-	27/7/17		Work on trenches continued, 61 yards being made ready for duckboarding. Fine. Quiet. Wiring continued on the Left front of MLR 120 yards & 350/12 and bell being done. A fighting patrol of 2nd Lieut F MUFF & 2nd Lieut J BUCKLEY left at 11.10 pm and reached pre-arranged positions at 11.45 pm at 11.45 pm Artillery 18 pdrs opened on sunken road from D 13 a 81 to D 8 c 41. The patrol then rushed the Crater at D 7 c 63; during this they advanced about 180 yards to within a few yards of enemy wire. Here made heavy fire a bombing encounter took place. Heavy barrage was encountered on the enemy who were also driven back on the front line into our artillery barrage from D 7 d 4 & 5 D 7 a 9. which was opened on them to cover our retirement. Congratulatory letter was received from the G.O.C. 186th Brigade. further reference to this patrol being given in appendix attached. Patrol returned at 3.30 am with four casualties, 2nd Lieut MUFF being slightly wounded. A protective patrol left C 18 a 78 at 11 pm of 2nd Lieut T H CHAMBERS and 6 O/R and discovered no enemy movement in front of our outposts.	Appendix MWS

WAR DIARY
or
INTELLIGENCE SUMMARY

(Erase heading not required.)

Army Form C. 2118

Place	Date	Hour	Summary of Events and Information	Remarks and references to Appendices
LYNE	28/7/17		Fine. Cont. a further 50 yards of French made ready for duckboards. Rest of day spent in. A patrol of 2nd Lieut (WHATTERS 2/-) and 6 O/R were out from 11pm to 2.45 am. Object reconnaissance to intercept any hostile patrols. Casualties to Patrol Nil. Enemy continued on M + R about 130 yards of wire put out.	Appx
-do-	29/7/17		Fine. Quiet. One casualty on line. wounded. Battalion relieved by 2/5th Bn. K.O.Y.L.I. Relief satisfactorily completed without casualties by 12.15 am, and Companies moved into encampments, to A Camp at 113 G 5 5. A patrol of 2nd Lieut A GOULD and 6 O/R out during relief as covering party.	Appx
A CAMP 113 G 5 5	30/7/17		Fine. Day spent on Interior economy. 2nd Lieut G. CARTWRIGHT took over duties of Adjutant to 185th Inf. Bgde School of Instruction.	Appx
-do-	31/7/17		Showery. Two Companies bathed and two Companies fired on A Range. remainder of Day spent on Inspection of rifles by Staff Armourer Sergeant and Close order drill.	Appx

W. Chamberlain
Lieut Col
Commanding
2/7th Bn Duke of Wellington's Regt.

2/7th Bn. Duke of Wellington's Regiment.

APPENDIX No. 1.

Divisional Routine Order No. 685 dated 9.7.1917.

HONOURS AND REWARDS. Under Authority granted by His Majesty the King, the Field Marshall Commanding-in-Chief, has awarded the following decoration to the undermentioned:-

THE MILITARY CROSS.

2nd Lieutenant HILTON FURNISS, Duke of Wellington's Regt.

for the following action:-

"On May 3rd, during the attack on BULLECOURT, in which the Duke of Wellington's Regiment took part, 2/Lieut. H. Furniss led his Platoon with dash and determination against a very heavy hostile machine gun and rifle fire. He was twice wounded, the second time severely in some fourteen places. In spite of this, he kept up in the enemy's wire with his men, encouraging and urging them to hold the line they then had until brought in at dusk by a stretcher party. He displayed a fine spirit on this occasion, greatly encouraging his men."

(Third Army A.M.S. H.R/585.)

2nd Lieutenant EDWARD TANNER, Duke of Wellington's Regt.

"On May 3rd, during the attack on BULLECOURT, in which the Duke of Wellington's Regiment took part, 2/Lieut. Tanner led his platoon with great determination and dash against a heavy hostile machine gun and rifle fire. He continued to show a fine spirit until wounded through the right eye which rendered him for the time being unconscious. On recovery he went forward, collecting some of his men, making a further attempt on the enemy front line. On this occasion he showed a fine example to his men."

(Third Army A.M.S. H.R/585.)

2/7th Bn. Duke of Wellington's Regiment.

APPENDIX No. 2.

Extract from 186th Infantry Brigade Summary of Intelligence, No. 12.

A Patrol in charge of 2/Lieut. MUFF together with 2/Lieut. BUCKLEY and 33 O.R., 2/7th. D of W's Regt., went out from left sub-sector at 10.30 p.m. yesterday, proceeded to C.12.d.7.8., thence N.W. to C.12.b.2.2. No enemy having been encountered, the patrol proceeded to ~~Cxk2xdxTxfxx~~ C.12.b.9.2. where an enemy post was suspected. This post was found to be occupied, was rushed and enemy driven out but no prisoners made. What appeared to be an aiming post (see attached sketch) was found under cover of a bank. This post was destroyed by bombs found there. The enemy was by this time firing on patrol from three sides and patrol therefore advanced in sectional rushes and the enemy retired to D.½.7.a.0.2., and then fell back gradually on his main line. Enemy trench mortar fire was then opened on patrol and rifle fire brought to bear on it from flanks. Patrol then retired 50 yards at a time. The enemy attempted to follow up but came under fire of covering party under Captain Alexander and at once retired.
Patrol heard a lot of movement of enemy transport in QUEANT and reports noise of what appears to be laying or tearing up of railway lines. It was further stated that No man's Land does not appear to be patrolled by the enemy.
Patrol returned at 3 a.m. Casualty Sgt. Allen, bayonet wound in leg. Notice boards in posts are forwarded herewith.

2/7th Bn. Duke of Wellington's Regiment.

APPENDIX No. 3.

Extract from 62nd Division Summary of Intelligence Summary. No. 30.

"An Offensive Patrol left C.18.b.5.4. at 11.10 p.m. to reconnoitre the CRATER and SUNKEN ROAD in D.7.c. Also if possible to secure an identification. Artillery co-operation protected the S. flank of patrol and diverted attention by firing on Road from D.13.a.8.1. to D.8.c.4.1. As patrol approached the Crater at D.7.c. 65.30 two enemy were seen to run towards their own wire. The Crater was rushed and found unoccupied. M.G. emplacement enfilading road towards LAGNICOURT was demolished. A fire step capable of holding a dozen men was also found. Our party came under heavy rifle fire from d.7.c.9.8. and advanced about 180 yards towards the enemy's main line where it was challenged by three sentry groups. A Very light revealed a large party of Germans running. This was attacked with Lewis Gun fire and bombs to which the enemy replied. Casualties were inflicted upon the enemy as they passed through their own wire at D.7.a.7.2. (10 or 12 were seen to fall). The offensive patrol came under heavy fire from all kinds of trench weapons. Also another hostile party of ± 10 was encountered and dispersed. By pre-arranged signal patrol obtained artillery support under cover of which they withdrew. Our casualties were one officer and three other ranks wounded. No identification was made as they heavy enemy fire made it impossible to approach further. Two unoccupied posts at D.7.c.85.70 having the appearance of converted shell holes were found. The enemy were caught under the protective artillery barrage from D.7.d.45.50 to D.7.a.9.2.

Officer i/c of patrol 2/Lieut. F. Muff Duke of Wellington's Regiment.

(COPY).

BMJ 16/3/114.

O.C. 2/7th. Bn. Duke of Wellington's Regt.

    I should like you to inform the Officers, N.C.O's and men who took part in last night's Operations how pleased I am at the dash and soldierly qualities displayed by all ranks. I am satisfied that every possible effort was made to secure an identification, and though this was not successful, your Patrols on this, as on the previous occasion, viz 24th, July, when a similar gallant attempt was made, have proved conclusively that Boche does not dominate "No Man's Land".

    I trust the experience gained during these Operations will encourage all ranks to further efforts.

                      (Sgd) F.F.HILL, Brig.Genl.
                              Cmdg 186th. Inf. Bde.

28.7.17.

Original

Vol 8

2/4th Bn. Duke of Wellington's Regt.

Secret War Diary

From:- 1st August 1914
To :- 31st August 1914

Rendered in accordance with F.S. Regs Part II

VOL VIII

W. Chambulin Lieut Colonel
              Commanding
2/4th Bn. Duke of Wellington's Regt.

Army Form C. 2118

WAR DIARY
or
INTELLIGENCE SUMMARY
(Erase heading not required.)

2/4th Duke of Wellingtons Regt

Place	Date	Hour	Summary of Events and Information	Remarks and references to Appendices
A CAMP I.13.b.55	1/8/17		Wet all day. Two Companies bathed and remainder occupied in Internal Economy Lectures. Staff Armourer Sergeant inspected Rifles. 2nd Lieut TH CHAMBERS attached to Bde 's Bgde REA for instruction. MC awarded to 2nd LIEUT (Temp/Lieut) AF GLOAG and 2/LIEUT (Temp LIEUT) E VAUGHAN. (DRO 747)	A.O
-do-	2/8/17		CAPTAIN R JAGGER of this Btn reports for duty after having been attached to 2/4th YORK & LANCS Regt. has given command of D Company during CAPTAIN JC ALEXANDERS absence on leave. CAPTAIN JC ALEXANDER went on leave. Rained all day. All parades cancelled. Armourer Sergeant inspected Rifles. O.C. Companies went to reconnoitre sector Bn. were to take over from the 2/5th WEST YORKS Regt.	A.O
-do-	3/8/17		Showery. Bn engages in preparations for relief. Battalion after being inspected by the Commanding Officer moved from Camp at 9.15 pm the following order C.B.A.D H.Q. to relieve the 2/5th WEST YORKS Regiment in the NOREUIL Sector. A Camp handed over to 2/5th WEST YORKS in good order and Defence Scheme received by him.	A.O
LINE	4/8/17		Relieved 2/5th WEST YORKS Regt in the NOREUIL Sector. Trenches muddy and flooded in parts. Relief completed 1.30am. Battn Headquarters at B.6.c.4.3.	A.O
-do-	5/8/17		Usual trench routine. Pumps obtained and trenches partially cleared of water. Men mostly engaged revetting and laying new duckboards.	A.O

WAR DIARY
or
INTELLIGENCE SUMMARY

(Erase heading not required.)

Army Form C. 2118

2/4th Duke of Wellingtons Regt

Instructions regarding War Diaries and Intelligence Summaries are contained in F.S. Regs., Part II. and the Staff Manual respectively. Title Pages will be prepared in manuscript.

Place	Date	Hour	Summary of Events and Information	Remarks and references to Appendices
LINE C.6.c.43	6/8/17		Fine day. Work progressed favourably. Minor patrol for identification purposes but no result. "D" Coy (in support) providing nightly working parties from front line. 30 men nightly as working party from 2/5th Dukes Regt.	WD
do	7/8/17		Wet most of the day. Trenches in bad condition and flooded in places. Aerial activity towards night. Situation generally quiet. Small patrols but no results of any moment.	WD
do	8/8/17		Quiet day. Usual trench routine. All available men engaged in clearing trenches. "A" Company relieved "D" Coy in the outpost position. Relief completed by dark.	WD
do	9/8/17		Showery. Laying of new trench boards proceeded with. Situation quiet. Transport shelled in NOREUIL at night. No casualties.	WD
-do-	10/8/17		Quiet day. Some rain. 2/Lieut A.A. GOULD admitted to hospital. Usual working parties. Small patrols. 1 man wounded.	WD
-do-	11/8/17		Trench routine. Machine gun activity at intervals. Lieut Sergt H. ORMEROD proceeded on leave. Enemy Minnies very active. Patrols small. 1 man killed.	WD

WAR DIARY or INTELLIGENCE SUMMARY

Army Form C. 2118

2/4th Duke of Wellington's Regt

Place	Date	Hour	Summary of Events and Information	Remarks and references to Appendices
LINE	12/8/17		Quiet day. Fine. Battalion relieved in line by 2/4th Y. and L. Regt. Relief completed satisfactorily at 1.45 a.m. on 13th. Battalion moved on relief to new "A" Camp MORY (B.28.c.9.4)	
"A" Camp MORY	13/8/17		Interior Economy. Men bathing at Divisional Baths, MORY. Camp very dirty. G.O.C. Division called at noon, men very tired.	A.H.Q.
—do—	14/8/17		Musketry on "A" Range. Strombos Horn established in camp. Baths again in use. Fine day. Ordinary training carried out.	A.H.Q.
—do—	15/8/17		Regimental routine. Range in use. Fairly large working parties. 25 men engaged daily on construction of winter stables.	A.H.Q.
—do—	16/8/17		Fine day. Camp now in clean and sanitary condition. 2/Lieut J. Maden arrived from hospital and posted to "D" Company.	A.H.Q.
—do—	17/8/17		Regimental Routine. Two companies bathing. Two companies firing on "A" Range. Fine day. Staff yearly Honours list prepared and submitted in draft form.	A.H.Q.

Army Form C. 2118.

WAR DIARY
or
INTELLIGENCE SUMMARY.
(Erase heading not required.)

2/4th Duke of Wellington's Regt

Instructions regarding War Diaries and Intelligence Summaries are contained in F. S. Regs., Part II. and the Staff Manual respectively. Title pages will be prepared in manuscript.

Place	Date	Hour	Summary of Events and Information	Remarks and references to Appendices
"A" Camp MORY	18/6/17		Fine day. Coy. Horse shew. 100 men from Battalion attended being conveyed from FAVREUIL by lorries. Orders received for taking up Southern Reserve position to the BULLECOURT Sector. Regtl Honours list completed and sent in to Brigade.	1/40
-do-	19/6/17		Strong as possible Church parade for 186th Infy Brigade at FAVREUIL. Battalion attended under Major R. MASON M.C. 1 man rated the C.O. and Lieut. G. WICKWOOD granted four days leave to PARIS and started by Motor at 2.30 p.m. Camp thoroughly cleaned in readiness to hand over to 2/5th WEST YORKS Regt.	1/40
-do-	20/6/17		2/5th WEST YORKS Regt. took over Southern Reserve position of BULLECOURT Sector at 9 p.m. and relieved 2/8th WEST YORKS Regt. Accommodation good. Tents and shelters. "A" Company located in ECOUST CAVES. "C" Company at CRAVCOURT. Headquarters and "B" and "D" Coy own outskirts of MORY. 2/Lieut A. MALLALIEU reported for duty from 34th Infantry Base Depot and posted to "D" Coy	1/40

Army Form C. 2118.

WAR DIARY
or
INTELLIGENCE SUMMARY.
(Erase heading not required.)

2/4 Duke of Wellingtons Regt

Place	Date	Hour	Summary of Events and Information	Remarks and references to Appendices
MORY	21/6/17		Battalion providing Working parties for O/Ls at ECOUST and VAULX. Fine day.	HQ
-do-	22/6/17		Working Parties. Accommodation of Battalion Headquarters improved. Draft of 32 other ranks received from Divnl Reinforcement Camp. s/Lt A.A. Gould discharged from hospital.	HQ
-do-	23/6/17		Showery. Working parties. s/Lt J.S. Clapham reported back from 6wks Haymaking Sector knives day and took over supervision of the Battalion winter stables	HQ
-do-	24/6/17		Usual working parties. The commanding Officer and Lieut C WLOCKWOOD returned from Paris	HQ
-do-	25/6/17		Orders received for taking over the left Sector at BULLECOURT. Working parties supplied. Wet day	HQ
-do-	26/6/17		Wet day. Company Officers attend Battalion in the line to arrange the relief by their Companies. Working parties as usual. Brigadier visited Headquarters.	HQ
-do-	27/6/17		Working parties still supplied	HQ

Army Form C. 2118.

WAR DIARY
or
INTELLIGENCE SUMMARY.
(Erase heading not required.)

2/4th Duke of Wellington's Regt

Place	Date	Hour	Summary of Events and Information	Remarks and references to Appendices
MORY	28/6/17		Billets cleaned ready for handing over. Battalion proceeded by companies independently to relieve the 2/5th Duke of Wellingtons Regiment in the BULLECOURT (left) sub sector. Headquarters "B" and "D" Coys conveyed to ECOUST on light Railway. Relief satisfactorily completed 1.30 a.m. Battalion Headquarters located at U 24 d 5.5. Both bdes attached	NO Appen
LINE	29/6/17		"A" and "B" Coys in front line "C" and "D" Coys in support the latter Coys supplying Working parties for the former. A patrol of Sgt A FIELD and 4 O.Rs proceeded to examine wire on the left of the road in U.21.d. Reported good condition – no casualties. Two other patrols under 2/Lt BICKLEY and 2/Lt QUARMBY respectively examined wire at U.21.c.4.6 and U.21.c.9.4 – reported good condition. Casualties – 1 O.Rk killed.	NO
–do–	30/6/17		Situation fairly quiet. Some french mortar activity. 2/Lt A MALLALIEU and 4 O.Rs proceeded to U.21.e.50.35. The sign of enemy were reported to be a strong 2/Lt STOTT and 4 O.Rs	NO

WAR DIARY or INTELLIGENCE SUMMARY.

Army Form C. 2118.

2/4th Duke of Wellington's Regt.

Place	Date	Hour	Summary of Events and Information	Remarks and references to Appendices
LINE	30/6/16	10 pm	Sentries proceeded to U 21 d 1.5 and U 21 d 15.45. Snipers on front close range. Owing to large number of lights sent up patrol withdrew. Capt ALEXANDER and 8 other ranks proceeded	H.Q
— do —	31/6/16	11.45am to U 21 c 9.4. Reported that enemy wire consisted of several belts of concertina mixed with barbed & wire but did not form a serious obstacle. No casualties on rest of front during day. Situation quiet. G.O.C. Division came round.	H.Q

M. Shankuhr Lieut Colonel
Cmdg.
2/4th Duke of Wellington's Regiment

APPENDIX No. ___

28.8.17.

BATTALION ORDER
by
LT. COLONEL F.G.CHAMBERLIN M.C. Commanding
2/7th Bn.Duke of Wellington's Regiment.
....

1. The 2/7th Bn.Duke of Wellington's Regiment will relieve the 2/5th Bn.Duke of Wellington's Regiment in the left sub-sector of BULLECOURT on the night of 28/29th August 1917.

2. On completion of relief the dispositions of Companies will be asfollows:-
   "A" Coy.   Right forward sector.
   "D" Coy.   Right support sector.
   "B" Coy.   Left forward sector.
   "C" Coy.   Left support sector.

3. O.C.Companies will make the necessary arrangements for guides etc with the Companies they relieve

4. Companies will pass the entrance to ECOUST at the following times:-
   "B" Coy.   10.0 p.m.
   "A" Coy.   10.15 p.m.
   "C" Coy.   10.30 p.m.
   "D" Coy.   10.45 p.m.
Usual distances between Platoons and Companies.

5. BULLECOURT AVENUE will be used only as an out trench during the relief.   Transport will use BULLECOURT-ECOUST Road.

6. All Trench Stores, Maps, Defence Schemes etc will be taken over and a list forwarded to Battn Headquarters by noon on the 29th August.
All work in hand and proposed work will be taken over to ensure continuity of work.

(1)

7. Completion of relief will be reported by the word "RAIN".

        /Sgd/ H% ORMEROD. Capt. & Adjutant.
        2/7th Bn. Duke of Wellington's Regt.

Copy No. 8. War Diary.

WR 9

Secret.

WAR DIARY
~of~
The 2/4th Bn. Duke of Wellington's (W.R) Regt.

From :- 1st September 1914
To :- 30th September 1914

J.W. Alexander
Capt. & major
commanding
2/4th Bn. Duke of Wellington's Regiment.

VOLUME IX

WAR DIARY or INTELLIGENCE SUMMARY

2/Yr Duke of Wellingtons Regt

Place	Date	Hour	Summary of Events and Information	Remarks and references to Appendices
LINE	1-9-17	10.40 P.M.	2/Lt A.E. Buckley and 3 O.R. left U.22.c.7.45. proceeded to U.22.c.7.4. U.22.c.8.4. U.22.c.8.2. The enemy wire seen from Rly. finished, concertina wire which has been badly knocked about, in-tact only for distance of few yards. Three red lights were seen from direction U.22.c.8.9. Whol. returned 1.15 A.M. No Casualties.	
"	"	11 P.M.	2/Lt A. Gallilleu and 5.O.R. left U.21.D.0.15. proceeded to U.21.D.0.45. A covering party of East Alexander and 14. O.R. When about 50 yards from the wire a small enemy digging party was heard at Lucitan Res trench, wire is about 4 yards wide and 4 ft high. Patrol returned 3 A.M. No Casualties	
"	"	11.30 P.M.	A Patrol consisting of 2/Lt d'Quarmby and 4.O.R. covered the ground between U.21.D.b.1 and U.21.D.9.4. and occupied M.G. emplacement at U.22.C.1.4. approx. Wire in front of Bowie trench appeared ? Enemy Artillery rather active. Enemy T.M. much quieter. returned 2.15 P.M. No Casualties	
"	2-9-17		2/Lt Plot and 6.O.R. left U.22.C.8.3 proceed to U.22.C.7.4. 2 enemy patrols were seen in the area patrolled, our party with Rifle fire and returned same route. Casualties Nil returned 2.15 A.M.	
"	"	11.35 P.M.	2/Lt Clifford and 6.O.R. patrolled area from U.21.C.8.1. U.21.C.8.5. U.21.C.9.9. The old wire annexed up behind his land badly smashed. There is a belt of wire about 6 yds. broad in front of the present enemy line. 2 Shots? coming of L.T. Register and 6.O.R. Casualties Nil returned 2.15 A.M.	
"	"	11.55 P.M.	Patrol led from U.22.C.8.3. proceeded north 160 yds, and returned same route. There is concertina wire at U.22.C.8.4. Enemy post in the old French trench behind his line. No Casualties returned 12.45. Weaker line.	

Army Form C. 2118.

WAR DIARY
or
INTELLIGENCE SUMMARY.   2/7th Duke of Wellington's Regt
(Erase heading not required.)

Place	Date	Hour	Summary of Events and Information	Remarks and references to Appendices
LINE	3-9-17	12 P.M.	Enemy observation balloons have been up throughout the day, enemy aeroplanes not much in evidence. Weather fine. 2/Lt Clifford and 6.O.R. Mort at 12 P.M., route U.21.C.9.b. to U.21.D.2.6, returning same route. Enemy wire reconnoitring in direction U.21.C.9.9, returned 2.15 A.M. Enemy T.M. rather quiet. Shells fell at U.22.c.8.3. No Casualties.	App
"	4-9-17		Throughout the night enemy T.M. have been more active than usual. Our aeroplanes rather active over enemy lines from 7 P.M. to 4:30 P.M. at a high altitude, engaged by enemy anti-aircraft guns. Enemy M.G. very quiet indeed. Weather fine. A patrol, consisting of 2/Lt Moth and 6.O.R. left U.22.c.8.2. at 12:15 AM proceeded to enemy post at U.22.c.8.3 approx found it unoccupied, proceeded N.W. about 60yds, enemy wire examined and found to consist of 1 belt of concertina wire, mixed with loose wire, enemy opened fire from Rifle and M.G. also fired from U.22.c.9.6 approx., enemy threw stick bombs from his trench, our patrol replied with Rifle & Mills Bombs. No Casualties	App
"	5-9-17		Weather fine. Enemy aircraft rather active. Battalion relieved in line by 2/5 K.O.Y.L.I. Relief completed satisfactorily at 11-45 P.M. Companies proceeded independently to "A" Camp. B.28.c.9.4. Mory. No Casualties. Relief order attached	Appendix
MORY	6-9-17		2 Lt Snuff admitted into Hospital. "A" and "B" Coys firing on "A" Range Weather fine. Instructions etc. "C" and "D"	App

WAR DIARY
INTELLIGENCE SUMMARY

2/7 Duke of Wellingtons Regt

Army Form C. 2118.

Place	Date	Hour	Summary of Events and Information	Remarks and references to Appendices
MORY (A.28.a.9.7) (FLYNN CAMP)	7-9-17		Coys. Musketry. Capt L Vaughan, Capt F Jagger and Capt G B Harker RAMC attend the 2nd period Officers Course at the Divisional Gas School. 2 P.L.I. Stafford attends Course at the VI Corps Bombing School at Gouvencourt-folle.	
—	8-9-17		Officers, N.C.Os and Men of "A" Coy attend Divisional Gas School. Lewis Gunners parade under 2/Lt Shaw. Musketry practice on rapid firing. Weather fine.	
—	9-9-17		Church of England Brigade Grenade device at B.10.B.55. Then rested during afternoon. Weather fine.	
—	10-9-17		Officers N.C.Os and Men of "B" Coy. attend Divisional Gas School. Extended order drill and skirmishing. Musketry practised. 2 Lt (Temp Lt) A Carborough appointed Intelligence Officer. Captain (Acting)	
—	11-9-17		Our M.O. Capt G E MARTIN leaves for July with No 29 C.C.S. Battalion parade at strong as possible for a Brigade Route March. Weather fine.	
—	12-9-17		Officers, N.C.Os and Men of "C" Coy. attend Divisional Gas School. Musketry exercised.	
—	13-9-17	8.30pm	Nine Companies at disposal of O.C. Coys. The battalion relieved the 2/8 West Yorks Regt in support in its right.	

WAR DIARY
INTELLIGENCE SUMMARY

Army Form C. 2118.

2/4 R Dukes of Wellingtons Regt

Place	Date	Hour	Summary of Events and Information	Remarks and references to Appendices
LINE	13.9.17		NOREUIL Sub-Section Battn H.Qrs at IGGAREE CORNER (C.10.b.6.0). B+C Coys in PONTEFRACT TRENCH. A Coy in Sunken road (Coy H.Qrs C.9.d.6.8.) D Coy at IGGAREE CORNER. 187 Brigade on our left. 58th Division on our right. Relief Complete 11.30 p.m. No casualties. Capt R.P.ANDERSON R.A.M.C. 2/3 F.A. attached for temporary duty as M.O. Capt JAGGER evacuated to hospital (sick). 2/Lt G.C. STOTT as P.E.O. Capt ALEXANDER & Lt LOCKWOOD leave for VALERY S SOMME. Capt GLOAG O.C. D Coy. Lt Col F.G. CHAMBERLIN M.C. C+G to ALBERT for 2 days Gas Course. MAJOR E.R. MASON M.C. in command of Unit.	Appendix 2.
	14.9.17		Fine. Battalion hospites. Working parties for work in front line under R.E. by night. 2/Lt T. BUCKLEY evacuated to hospital (slightly wounded by bullet in right leg.)	9.16 9.16
	15.9.17		Fine. Artillery clearing & improving trenches, putting in wire racks etc. & providing working parties for R.E. at night. 2 R.I.F. MADEN reports for duty from leave & is attached to B Coy for duty.	9.16
	16.9.17		Fine. Working parties for R.E. Lieut. HAR. SMEED about 5 wells nothing around to come.	9.16
	17.9.17		Fine. C O visits H.Qrs for 24 hours. R.S.M. WORKING parties for R.E. A Coy party under 2/Lt CHAMBERS shelled with 77 mm Sgt GLEDHILL killed & L/Cpl wounded.	9.16
	18.9.17		Fine. C.O goes to Transport Lines en route for leave. 2/Lt A MALAVIEU evacuated to hospital (sick). Brig-Genl F.F HILL encloses transfer working parties for R.E.	9.16

Army Form C. 2118.

WAR DIARY
or
INTELLIGENCE SUMMARY. 7th Duke of Wellington's Regt
(Erase heading not required.)

Instructions regarding War Diaries and Intelligence Summaries are contained in F.S. Regs., Part II. and the Staff Manual respectively. Title pages will be prepared in manuscript.

Place	Date	Hour	Summary of Events and Information	Remarks and references to Appendices
LINE	19.9.17		FINE. Working parties for R.E. Lt C Pogson evacuated to hospital (sick) 2 Coy bathing at battalion H.Q.	
"	20.9.17		FINE. More working parties for R.E. 2 Cp baths at B. Ham Cy Cars up line.	
"	21.9.17		FINE. Battalion relieved by Companies independently to relieve the 2/5th Duke of Wellington's Regt in the Reserve Sub Section NOREUIL. Relief very methodically & quickly carried out. Complete without casualties at 10.0 pm. Batt. H.Q. located at Chardelehaden. Battn order attached. Battalion boundary from U 23 6.5.05 to U 29 b.6.85. In touch with the 2/7th West Yorkshire Regt on our right & to 2/4th Duke of Wellington's Regt on our Left. 2/Lt E. Tanner reports for duty & is attached to "C" Coy.	
"	21.9.17		FINE. A.5" Trench mortar dumped h.e. toxic shells & China S mortar bombs near C3 Brigade wash and damage to D.E. dm. H.D. 6.14 schms. All C.G Allport + 14 o.k. left 0.33/14 hours at ours on returning some hours at 11.45 am. Patrols state around very hard out up by shell holes L/Cpl B. West & 2 others wounded whilst making a Lewis Post.	

WAR DIARY or INTELLIGENCE SUMMARY

Army Form C. 2118.

2/7th Duke of Wellington Regt

Place	Date	Hour	Summary of Events and Information	Remarks and references to Appendices
LINE	23/9/17		FINE 4+6" trench in HORSE SHOE Support deepened & widened. Trenches all over knee latrines put in strong posts 3 coils of wire 7 knife rests put out. Sgt WATERS - 4 O.R. left U23d10.05 at 9.0pm returning Same way at 11.0pm after having reconnoitred the ground U23c 75.25 Sgt Taylor & left D9/11 to recce at 8.30pm returned to U23 b 45 & U29 d 08 returning to U29/2 near a 11.0pm no enemy seen recently	9/16
"	24/9/17		FINE A little shelling of our front. 4.6" gunes in HORSE SHOE received a Whizz from posts U.23/18. U23/D & U29/B 2E about 30° Later. 3 Knife rests out at U29b.62 2nd Lt ETANNER + 15 O.R. left posn U29/5 E at 10.30pm returning same posn at 11.30pm Patrol reached U23d.75.15 whence they had to return under bomb attacks. No Casualties. One O.R. killed in line.	9/16
"	25/9/17		FINE our artillery carrying out shoots. Active shelling of enemy TM's & great activity on part of enemy MGs. 20° of lost learning /wirecut in front of U23/5 & next B" in part of U29/5. A hour at dusk arrival of 30 O.R. (8 for A Coy - 12 for B Coy - 4 for C Coy - 6 for D Coy) very good men mostly of previous service in France. D & C Coy still satisfactorily completed	9/16

Army Form C. 2118.

WAR DIARY or INTELLIGENCE SUMMARY.
(Erase heading not required.) 2/y R Duke of Wellington's Regt

Place	Date	Hour	Summary of Events and Information	Remarks and references to Appendices
LINE	25/4/17		Rels. by 7.30 p.m. On completion of relief "A" Coy were in the APEX. "B" Coy on right. "D" Coy in PUDSEY SUPPORT & "C" Coy in HORSE SHOE REDOUBT. Forward posts were to be cleared from 10.0 a.m. to 4.30 p.m. Our artillery bombarding enemy trenches. No casualties.	
—	26/4/17		FINE. Barrage on our lines as retaliation for our half hour barrage on enemy trenches from 5.30 to 6.0 a.m. Only slight damage to trenches. 4 men slightly wounded. 20" wire put out between posts U23b79 to U23b7-30'. Reconnaissance wire in front of U29/5.9. Clearing trenches & rearranging posts commenced. 2nd Lt ETANNER & 2nd Lt HAYWARD & 180R. left U23/3 at about 2.0 a.m. & proceeded to U23d16 where the enemy wire was found to be strongly staked. Patrol returned. No casualties at 4.0 a.m. Sgt K ALLEN & 7 O.R. after U29 b 55.05 at 12.15 a.m. & proceeded to 20.9.NE returned 3 a.m./4 a.m. at 2.15 a.m. No casualties. No enemy seen. 1 O.R. wounded.	
—	27/4/17		FINE. Very Quiet. Capt ALEXANDER. M.C. & Lt. C. LOCKWOOD & two unidentified parties of O. ranks R.E. & FEARN & 5 O.R. went out at 8.15 & 10.30 p.m from U29/5.2 & after to U29 b 55.05 & U28 d.45.40 & straight wires put at U23 a 25. Found wire empties. No casualties.	

T2134. Wt. W708-776. 500000. 4/16. Sir J.C. & S.

WAR DIARY or INTELLIGENCE SUMMARY

Army Form C. 2118.

1/7 Duke of Wellington's Regt

Place	Date	Hour	Summary of Events and Information	Remarks and references to Appendices
LINE	27.9.17		Patrol of 2Lt G. HATTERSLEY & 2nd Lt T. MADEN & 16 O.R. left W29/1 A hour at 11 pm and Consolidated Shellhole at U30 c 2.1 Unoccupied but showing signs of recent occupation. Proceeded to U30 a 3 4 where they were challenged. Attempted to outflank but held up by strong enemy wire. Patrol forced to return to Crawick. Remnant made it U29/50 hour all ranks accounted for. 20 wounds & 25 french wire put out. Four other ranks wounded. G.O.C. visited line.	
	28.9.17		Fine. Very quiet. HPE shelled from 3.45 to 4.45 pm. Patrol of 2Lt ALLEN & 5 O.R. left U29/5A at 7.10pm to Crawick from every hour at U29 b 75 70. however 1610 yards [?] were fine. Enemy Lewis strong. Lewis definitely heard enemy patrol but withdrew. O.S.C. returned 8 o/m to Crawick. 1 B.R. committed attached. Line = inflicted casualties. Party returned 8 o/m to Crawick. 1 O.R. wounded	Appendix 3
	29.9.17		Fine. Very quiet. 1 O.R. wounded. Relieved in line by 2/5 York & Lancaster Regt. Relief completed satisfactorily by 10 o/m. Covering patrol of 2/5 STAFFORD & Gol to Crawick. Companies proceeded independently to H Camp Relief order attached	Appendix 4
H Camp	30.9.17		Fine. Very quiet day. Battalion rested morning. Bath afternoon. 2 Lt J.F. HARTLEY & 6 SMITH reported for duty. Capt H. ORMEROD admitted to hospital	
(U28 c 9.7)				

Habergham
Major
off 1. Comdg
2/7 Duke of Wellington's Regt

War Diary ① *Secret*

BATTALION ORDERS
by
LIEUT. COLONEL. F.G.CHAMBERLIN M.C. COMMANDING
2/7th Bn. DUKE of WELLINGTON'S REGIMENT.
IN THE FIELD.   WEDNESDAY.   5. 9. 1917.
....

1. The Battalion will be relieved in the Line on the night September 5/6th 1917 by the 2/5th Bn. K.O.Y.L.I.

2. All details of relief and arrangements for guides, other than those ordered herein, will be arranged direct by Company Commanders with the Company Commanders of the relieving Unit.

3. All Trench Maps, Aeroplane photographs, Defence Schemes and Trench Stores will be handed over and a receipt taken. A copy of all Trench Stores handed over will be handed to Orderly Room immediately in arrival in Camp. All work in hand and proposed work, with Maps, will be carefully handed over.

4. The Quartermaster will take over accommodation at "A" Camp MORY (B.28.c.9.7.). C.Q.M.Ss will accompany him to take over the accommodation of their Companies. All men's packs, Officers' Valises etc will be taken there on the 5th inst. to be in readiness. Companies on relief, will proceed independently to "A" Camp. Usual intervals between Platoons will be observed.

5. The Transport Officer will provide Limbers as under to be at the ration dump by 10.45 p.m.:-
Headquarters - 2 limbers.
Medical Officer - 1 limber.
"B" and "D" Coys. - 1 limber each.
The following limbers will be the ration dump

(1)

at 12 midnight:-
"A" and ~~XX~~ "C" Coys:- 1 limber each.

6. No. 1 Lewis Gunners will proceed with their respective Company Limbers to take charge of the guns and ammunition.

7. Company Officers will report the arrival of their Companies in "A" Camp immediately, stating the time on such report.

8. Orders for bathing on 6th inst. have been circulated to all concerned under separate cover.

9. Acknowledge.

H Ormerod Captain & Adjutant.
2/7th Bn. Duke of Wellington's Regiment.

Copies to:-
"A" Coy.
"B" Coy.
"C" Coy.
"D" Coy.
Transport Officer.
Quartermaster.
Medical Officer.
R.S.M.
War Diary.

BATTALION ORDERS
by
LIEUT-COLONEL F.G. CHAMBERLIN, M.C., C de G., COMMANDING
2/7th. Bn. DUKE OF WELLINGTON'S REGIMENT.

IN THE FIELD.   WEDNESDAY.   12th. SEPTEMBER 1917.

1. The Battalion will relieve the 2/8th. Bn. West Yorkshire Regiment (in Reserve) in the right HORSHOE Sub-Section on the night of 13/14th. September 1917.

2. Company Officers will proceed to the line this afternoon to make the necessary arrangements direct with the Company Officers whom they relieve.
   "A" Coy will relieve "A" Coy of the 2/8th. Bn. West Yorkshire Regt.
   "B" Coy will relieve "B" Coy of the 2/8th. Bn. West Yorkshire Regt.
   "C" Coy will relieve "C" Coy of the 2/8th. Bn. West Yorkshire Regt.
   "D" Coy will relieve "D" Coy of the 2/8th. Bn. West Yorkshire Regt.
   All details other than those ordered herein will be arranged between O.C.Companies concerned.

3. The head of the first Company will pass the VAUX-ST.LEGER ROAD at 9.10 p.m. to-morrow night.   Movement east of this Road will be by Platoons with intervals.

4. O.C.Companies will make their own arrangements with the Transport Officer as to transport required.

5. All Trench Maps, Trench Stores, Aeroplane Photographs, Defence Schemes, etc. will be taken over.   All work on hand and proposed work (with maps) will be carefully taken over to ensure continuity of work.   A duplicate copy of all Trench Stores will be forwarded to Battalion Headquarters by 8 a.m. on the 1st., instant.

6. Completion of relief will be reported to Battalion Headquarters in BAB Code immediately each Company relief is completed.

7. Indents for R.E. material will be forwarded to Orderly Room by 6 p.m. each night for delivery on the following night.

8. If any Preserved Meat and Biscuits are taken over as Trench Stores for use as Emergency Rations, a Report will be rendered on the quantity and condition of these by 6 p.m. on the 14th. instant.

9. Salvage Dumps will be formed at Coy Headquarters and material from these Dumps will be sent back nightly by the Ration Wagons and disposed of by the Transport Officer in accordance with instructions which will be issued to him.   The Brigade Salvage Squad will be attached to the Battalion and will assist in the collection of Salvage.

10. Particulars of Guards and duties which will be found by the Battalion will be given to the R.S.M., and will make the necessary arrangements.

11. Blankets will be folded in bundles of 10 and stacked, along with men's packs, opposite the end of each Company lines by 8 p.m. to-morrow.
    Officers' Valises will also be ready by 4 p.m. to-morrow.
    O.C.Companies will arrange for their Officers' kits to be ready for removal as soon as possible.

12. The Camp will be thoroughly cleaned during to-morrow and Certificates rendered by Companies to Orderly Room that the billets occupied by the men under their Command are left in a clean and sanitary condition.

                                (sgd) R. ORMEROD, Capt. & Adjt.,
                                   2/7th. Bn. Duke of Wellington's Regt.

(3)

BMJ 16/3/175.

To O.C. 2/7th. Duke of Wellington's Regt.

The G.O.C. Brigade has read with great interest the report of the patrol carried out under Sgt. ALLEN H., on the night of the 28th/29th. September, and has made the following remarks :-

"Very good work, patrol to be informed."

(Sgd) G. WINGFIELD STRATFORD, Captain,
Brigade Major,
186th. Infantry Brigade

29.9.17.

BATTALION ORDERS
by
MAJOR E.R.MASON M.C. COMMANDING
2/7th Bn. Duke of Wellington's Regiment.

In the Field.   Thursday.   September 27th 1917.

....

1. The Battalion will be relieved in the Line on the night of September 29/30th 1917 by the 2/5th Bn. York and Lancaster Regiment.

2. Company Commanders from the relieving Unit will be visiting Companies to-morrow and details of relief, other than those contained herein, will be arranged direct.

3. Guides for each Platoon will be sent to Battalion Headquarters by 4.0 p.m. on Saturday September 29th and will receive their instructions here.

4. All Trench Stores, Maps, Aeroplane photographs, defence schemes etc. will be handed over and a receipt obtained. A duplicate of this list will be forwarded to Orderly Room by 6 a.m. on the 30th inst. All work in hand, and proposed work (with maps) will be carefully handed over.

5. On relief, Companies will move independently to "A" Camp. Usual distances will be observed between Platoons. Arrival in camp will be at once notified to Orderly Room and the time of arrival stated on the message.

6. The transport Officer will arrange the necessary transport required for each Company and Headquarters, and will notify them of his arrangements.

7. The Quartermaster will take over "A" Camp on the afternoon of the 29th inst. C.Q.M.Sgts will accompany him to take over the accommodation for their respective Companies.

8. Blankets packs etc will be in readiness for distribution on arrival. Officers' valises will also be in readiness.

9. Completion of relief in the line will be reported to Battalion Headquarters immediately by the word "APPLE".

10. SYDNEY AVENUE will be used as an "Out trench" only during the relief except in the case of heavy shelling.

11. Acknowledge.

/Sgd/ G. A. CARTWRIGHT. 2/Lieut. & A/Adjt.
2/7th Bn. Duke of Wellington's Regiment.

Copies to :-
"A" Company.
"B" Company.
"C" Company.
"D" Company.
Transport Officer & Quartermaster.
War Diary.

Sidney

SECRET.

2/7th. BN. DUKE OF WELLINGTON'S REGIMENT.

WAR DIARY.

1st. OCTOBER 1917
- to -
31st. OCTOBER 1917.

Volume X.

E. Chamberlain   Lieut. Colonel
                  Commanding
2/7th. Bn. Duke of Wellington's Regiment.

Army Form C. 2118.

WAR DIARY
or
INTELLIGENCE SUMMARY.
(Erase heading not required.)

2/7 Duke of Wellington Regt

Place	Date	Hour	Summary of Events and Information	Remarks and references to Appendices
MORY (H'Camp) B2&c 9.1	1.10.17	MORN	FINE. Field firing on "C" Range. Batting. 2nd Lt H M SMITH reported for duty. 2nd LT J.S. CLAPHAM rejoined from ETAPLES for duty. 2nd LT GAOHART Right acting Adjutant	See App 6
-do-	2.10.17		FINE. A & B Coys Interior Economy C & D Coys Field firing on "C" range.	See App 6
-do-	3.10.17		FINE. Field firing on "C" Range	See App 6
-do-	4.10.17		FINE. Batta Drill & training for Coys shorts. A lecture was given to Officers & NCOs by the Corps O.C. Pigeons.	
-do-	5.10.17		WET. Coys hating at FAVREUIL. & Coy inspected by the Assister General by GENL BRAITHWAITE & Army Inspector of Physical Training.	See App 6
-do-	6.10.17		WET. LT W H HOUSE U.S.M.C. reports as Medical Officer. 20# took in PONTRACT TRENCH 146	
-do-	7.10.17		WET. The morning was devoted to cleaning up killus, packing etc. The Battalion was aroused at 5+5pm to proceed to relief the 2/4 th York & Lancaster Regt in the Right NOREUIL Sub section. Relief successfully Completed at 11.0pm in pouring rain. All four Companies in front lines from left to right - B.A.C. & D Coys. The trenches were in a dirty condition. Bn HDQRS at C11.C.6.9. Left Battalion Boundary U29.a.8. Right Boundary C11.a.2.7	# Appendix 1

WAR DIARY or INTELLIGENCE SUMMARY.

Army Form C. 2118.

2/7 DUKE OF WELLINGTONS

Place	Date	Hour	Summary of Events and Information	Remarks and references to Appendices
In the LINE	7/10/17		The 2/5 Bn DUKE of WELLINGTONS in the LEFT NOREUIL Sub Section to the 1/4th LONDON Regt. on our right. A Patrol of 2nd Lieut T. CLAPHAM & 8 O.R. left Coy H.Q. 1 hour at 12.30 am 8/10/17 proceeded to Sunken Road O6.c.3.1 along our wire to O5.d.1 hours & contacted Rey Culty in O6.a. Midway Pte SLATER was wounded. The officer 4/c 202 & 610 Pte SHEPHERD. with him returned to our hour O14/2 at 3.30 am for a stretcher. On proceeding to the spot where the men had been left, no trace could be found.	Sub
—	8/10/17		Wet. Search continued for missing men. Our front quiet. & batteries 2nd Lt. G. HATTERSLEY & 2nd Lt J. MADEN & 13 O.R. from C14/2 hour at 2.15 am returning to C14/2 hour at 4.45 am. to search for missing men. 2nd Lieut. C.O. STOTT & 6 O.R. 4/c Rey Culty in O5d Exit 11.30pm & returned, and saw 1.30 am Report that the enemy liaison hour at O6d1.b was not occupied. 2nd Lt. T. BUCKLEY & 5 O.R. left C14/1 hour at 8.30pm & returned to same hour at 11 Cpm. after having searched ground he found no trace of missing men. 2nd Lt H. THORNTON & 8 O.R. left U29 d.8.1. at 2.6 am returning to U29 d.9.1 at 4.0 am. having patrolled our front returned there down. No casualties.	Sub

WAR DIARY
INTELLIGENCE SUMMARY
2/7 Duke of Wellington's Regt.

Place	Date	Hour	Summary of Events and Information	Remarks and references to Appendices
In the Line	9/10/17		FINE. Quiet. 2 O.R. wounded. 3 Patrols out covering the front & scouting for missing men. 2/Lt T. BUCKLEY & 9 O.R. left C5/1/2 hour at 8.30pm returning to same hour at 11.30pm. Patrol reached Crater at C6d 5.8 unoccupied. Investigated wired with a gap acts SE side. 2/Lt J.S. QUARMBY & 11 O.R. left C11 a 1.0 at 10.45pm & returned to C5A 8.6 at 1.10am having thoroughly searched the ground in front of our posts. 2/Lt A.W. SMITH & 6 O.R. left C5d q.5 at 1.10am & returned to same point at 3.45am. Patrol proceeded to Crater at C6d 5.8 via mine at C6c+3o Crow Roads at C6aq5.40. Crater unoccupied.	S/b
—	10.10.17		WET. Lt Col F.S. CHAMBERLIN MC CMG returns from leave. Our front quiet. The Battalion was relieved from the Right NOREUIL Sub Section by the 18th Battn Northumberland Fusiliers. Relief complete at 10.25 pm. Companies proceeded independently to 'A' Camp (B28097)	Appendix 2 S/b S/b
—	11.10.17		FINE. Companies resting in morning & cleaning all kits.	
—	12.10.17		WET. The Battalion paraded at 12.45 pm to leave FAVREUIL AREA. Marched to 'C' Camp (M18c4.1) BEAUMONT AREA & relieved the 1st Battn Royal Scots Fusiliers. The battalion accommodated in wooden huts & a	Appendix 3

WAR DIARY
or
INTELLIGENCE SUMMARY.

Army Form C. 2118.

2/7 DUKE OF WELLINGTONS

Place	Date	Hour	Summary of Events and Information	Remarks and references to Appendices
C.Camp (N.18.c.4.1)	12.10.17		Very satisfactory camp. The afternoon was spent by the men in getting their things dry. Major E.C. MASON M.C. on course at ALBERT.	Apps
-do-	13.10.17		FINE. Day spent in settling in & inspection of clothing etc. 2 Lt N.T. ARGH reported for duty & is posted to D Coy.	Apps
-do-	14.10.17		FINE. Church Service. Lieut. W.C. POGSON joins the Bn. as BOARDING Officer. 2 Lt G. HATTERSLEY is appointed LEWIS GUN Officer. Capt. R.P. ANDERSON returns from leave - relieves Lt W.H. HOUSE U.S.M.C. as our Medical Officer. Capt. A.F. GLOAG M.C. leaves for ENGLAND on leave.	Apps
-do-	15.10.17		FINE. The following Officers are entitled to the rank of LIEUTENANT, with effect from the respective dates on which they complete 18 months Commissioned Service:- 2Lts G. CLIFFORD - T. MADEN - A. PEARSON - T.H. CHAMBERS - E. DAVIES - E. TANNER M.C. - T. ROPP - A. HAYTHORNE - H.E.D. WALKER - G.A. SHAW - T. HAWKSFIELD - A. MALLALIEU - C.G. STOTT - H.L. HOPPER - S.P. HAYWARD - L. KERSHAM E. FURN 16th M.C. 2/Lt (acting Captain) H. ORMEROD - T. VAUGHAN M.C. A.F. GLOAG M.C. Day spent in re-organising platoons.	Apps Apps
-do-	16.10.17		FINE. Practice attacks etc.	
-do-	17.10.17		FINE. Platoons in attack & battling. Major E.C. MASON M.C. evacuated to hospital.	

Army Form C. 2118.

WAR DIARY
or
INTELLIGENCE SUMMARY.
(Erase heading not required.)

2/7 DUKE OF WELLINGTON'S

Place	Date	Hour	Summary of Events and Information	Remarks and references to Appendices
"C" Camp (N18c4.1)	17.10.17		Lecture to all officers at 4.0pm by the Divisional Commander.	946
	18.10.17		FINE. Companies in the attack. Medical inspection by the M.O.	946
—	19.10.17		FINE. Firing on "L" Range & Companies in the attack. Capt (tepy) H. ORMEROD evacuated to hospital. LT W.E POGSON took over duties as ADJUTANT.	946
—	20.10.17		FINE. Morning. Companies took P.T. & B.F & rapid wiring. Half Holiday for afternoon. Football matches played.	946
—	21.10.17		FINE. Brigade parade. Church service at 11.0 am	946
—	22.10.17		FINE. 2 Companies on I range & remainder Close & Extended Order drill etc. F.C.C.M. on No 305212 Sgt Taylor J & No 305449 L/C Sutcliffe H. Both found NOT GUILTY. 2nd Lts Y.G.W. PEPPER, A. HINCHCLIFFE, T.D. JOHNSTON report for duty. Came from K.A.R.G.C Coys respectively	946
—	23.10.17		WET. Lectures in morning. Specialists training in afternoon. Lecture to all officers from 5.30 pm on Recent Ranges by Brigade Major R.A	946
—	24.10.17		WET. Coy Exercise forming up on tape. "A" Coy on R Range. Bathing in afternoon. Lecture to Officers at 6.0 pm on Communications by Div O.C Signals.	946
—	25.10.17		WET. Battalion exercise in lining up on tape field firing in afternoon	946

T2134. Wt. W708—776. 500000. 4/15. Sir J.C.&S.

Army Form C. 2118.

WAR DIARY
or
INTELLIGENCE SUMMARY.
(Erase heading not required.)

2/7 Duke of Wellington's Regt

Instructions regarding War Diaries and Intelligence Summaries are contained in F. S. Regs., Part II. and the Staff Manual respectively. Title pages will be prepared in manuscript.

Place	Date	Hour	Summary of Events and Information	Remarks and references to Appendices
"C" Camp (N18 C + I)	26.10.17		WET. Brigade exercise in lining up on tape. 2/7th supporting 2/5 Bn D. of W. Regt. Very successful. Evening exercise washed out owing to heavy rain	
—	27.10.17		FINE. 2nd Lt J.S. CLAPHAM to England for leave. Rapid Wiring & Consolidation of shell hole by "B" "C" Coys on L range. 2nd Lt C.C. PODSON at Lewis gun firing rg. posts & 2 Coy	Ggb
—	28.10.17		FINE. Church Parade at 10.30 am. Afternoon spent in sports etc	Ggb Ggb
—	29.10.17		FINE. Battalion fatigue clearing camp & packing stores etc	Ggb
—	30.10.17		FINE morning. Parade at 7.0 am for move to COURCELLES. Arrive at "B" Camp (A19c6.5) at 11.10 am. WET in afternoon.	APPENDIX 4 Ggb
GOUY-EN-ARTOIS (O19a)	31.10.17		FINE. Battalion moves off at 6.30 am for GOUY-EN-ARTOIS via AYETTE-DOUCHY- AYETTE-ADINFER-RANSART-BELLACOURT-BEAUMETZ-WANCHIET. Reach billets at 1.50 pm. Battalion complimented on its appearance & discipline whilst on march by G.O.C. 186 Inf. Brigade. Men accommodated in huts in huts & officers in the former Citadelle. Batt Hqrs at Bille 93 RUE D'ARRAS.	APPENDIX 5 Ggb Ggb

T. Chamberlain
Lt Colonel
Comdg 2/7 Duke of Wellington's Regt

31.10.17

APPENDIX 1

BATTALION ORDERS
by
MAJOR E.R. MASON, D.S.O., COMMANDING
2/7th. BN. DUKE OF WELLINGTON'S REGIMENT.

IN THE FIELD.   SATURDAY.   6th. OCTOBER 1917.
....

1. The Battalion will relieve the 2/4th. Bn. York & Lancs Regt. in the Right Sub-Section of the Right (MORTUIL) Section on the night of the 7/8th. October.

2. All details of relief, other than those ordered herein, will be arranged direct by O.C. Companies with the O.C. Companies of the Unit to be relieved.

3. Companies will relieve Companies of the 2/4th. Bn. York & Lancs Regt. as under :-
   'A' Coy 2/7th. D.of W.Regt. will relieve 'D' Coy 2/4th. Y & L. Regt.
   'B' Coy   do.   do.   will relieve 'C' Coy   do.   do.
   'C' Coy   do.   do.   will relieve 'A' Coy   do.   do.
   'D' Coy   do.   do.   will relieve 'B' Coy   do.   do.

4. The 2 Anti-Aircraft Lewis Gun Guards at ENTRACMENT will rejoin their Companies on relief to-morrow afternoon.

5. All Trench maps, Trench Stores, Aeroplane Photographs and Defence Schemes will be taken over. All work in hand and proposed work, with maps, will be carefully taken over to ensure continuity of work. A copy of all Trench Stores, including Bombs (by classes) S.A.A., etc., will be rendered to Battalion Headquarters by 6 a.m. on the 8th. instant.

6. Completion of relief will be reported to Battalion Headquarters by the code word "BOX".

7. Movement east of VAUX-St.LEGER ROAD will be by Platoons with intervals and road must not be crossed before 7.30 p.m.

8. Platoon Guides will be at the railway crossing at the entrance to MORCHIES at 8.15 p.m.

9. O.C. 'C' and 'D' Companies will arrange for their working parties of 1 Officer and 50 Other Ranks to move forward from PONTEFRACT TRENCH to be in readiness for the relief.

10. Men will proceed up the line in Marching Order with Overcoats in the Packs.

11. Blankets, Coy Stores, Mess Kits, Boxes, Valises, etc. will be in readiness for the Transport, as far as possible, by 2 p.m. to-morrow.

12. O.C. Companies will make their own arrangements with the Transport Officer regarding Transport required for the Line.

                          (Sgd) C.A. CARTWRIGHT, 2/Lieut. & A/Adjt.,
                                2/7th. Bn. Duke of Wellington's Regiment.

APPENDIX 2

3/7th. BN. DUKE OF WELLINGTON'S REGT.

ORDER NO. 5.

9th. October 1917.

1. This Unit will be relieved in the Right (NOREUIL) Sub-Section by the 1st. Bn. Northumberland Fusiliers Regt. on the night of the 10/11th. October 1917.

2. 1 Officer per Company (as already detailed) and 1 N.C.O. per Platoon will be left in the Trenches for 24 hours after completion of relief.

3. All details of relief, other than those ordered herein, will be arranged direct between Company Commanders concerned.

4. All Trench Stores, Maps, Aeroplane Photographs and Defence Schemes will be handed over on relief and a copy of Receipt will be forwarded to Battalion Headquarters by 9.0 a.m. on the 11th. instant.
All work in progress and proposed work (with Maps) will be carefully taken over.

5. 4 Guides per Company will report at Battalion Headquarters at 7.15 p.m. to-morrow, 10th. instant, these to act as Platoon Guides to meet incoming Unit at cross-roads at the NOREUIL CEMETERY at C.16.a.4.4. at 8.0 p.m.
2/Lieut. A.V.Spafford will report at Battalion Headquarters at 7.15 p.m. to-morrow, 10th. instant, to act as Officer i/c Guides.

6. 1 Limber for 'A' Coy and 1 Limber for 'B' Coy will report at 'A' and 'B' Companies joint ration dump at 9.0 p.m.
1 Limber for 'C' Coy and 1 Limber for 'D' Coy will report at 'C' and 'D' Companies' joint ration dump at 9.0 p.m.
2 Limbers for Headquarters Coy and Medical Stores will report at Battalion Headquarters at 8.0 p.m.
Company Commanders' Riding Horses will be at C.16.a.4.4. at 9.45 p.m.

7. On relief, Companies will proceed independently to 'A' Camp.

8. An Advance Party of the 4 Company Quartermaster Sergeants and Sgt. Green H. will report to the Quartermaster, who will take over 'A' Camp in the afternoon of the 10th. instant.

9. Completion of relief will be notified to Battalion Headquarters by the code word 'RATION' and arrival in 'A' Camp reported immediately to Battalion Headquarters.

10. Movement East of the VAUX-VRAUCOURT-St.LEGER ROAD will be by Platoons with intervals.

11. SYDNEY AVENUE will be used as an out-trench only during relief except in case of heavy shelling.

12. ACKNOWLEDGE.

(Sgd) G.A.CARTWRIGHT, 2/Lieut. & A/Adjt.,
3/7th. Bn. Duke of Wellington's Regiment.

War Diary

APPENDIX 3

ADMINISTRATIVE ORDERS
for
MOVE TO BEAULENCOURT AREA ON 12. 10.17
by
LIEUT.COLONEL F.G.CHAMBERLIN M.C. C. de G. COMMANDING
2/7th Bn. DUKE of WELLINGTN'S REGIMENT.
....

1. THE Battalion will move on October 12th 1917 yo "C" Camp (N.18.c.4.1.) BEAULENCOURT AREA, at present occupied by 1st Battalion, Royal Scots Fusiliers.

2. TRANSPORT Lines will be taken over from their corresponding Unit.

3. WATER Point. N.24.d.2.9.
   Horses.   N.24.d.2.9.

4. TWO Baggage Wagons will report at Headquarters at 7.0 a.m. All Stores and Officers' Valises will be at the end of Company Lines at that time.

5. O.C. "B" Company will detail two men to report to Brigade Headquarters at 6.50 a.m. to guide two Motor Lorries to Battalion Headquarters.

6. ADVANCE Parties:- 2/Lieut. E. Tanner and two other ranks per Company (including Headquarters Company) will report at Brigade Headquarters at 7.0 am. to act as Advance Party.

7. REAR Party:- 2/Lieut. J. Maden and two other ranks per Company (one to be a N.C.O.) and two other ranks of Headquarters, will remain behind as rear party. Receipts will be taken for all stores handed over and a Certificate obtained from the Area Commandant, that the Camp and Transport Lines are left in a clean and sanitary condition.

8. 2/Lieut. A.B.Smith, will reconnoitre the route to the new quarters to-day. He will report to Headquarters at 2.0 p.m.

9. ORDERS for parade willbe issued later.

/Sgd/ H. ORMEROD. Captain & Adjutant.
2/7th Bn.Duke of Wellington's Regiment.

In the Field.
11. 10. 1917.

APPENDIX 4

BATTALION ORDERS
by
LIEUT.COLONEL F.G.CHAMBERLIN.M.C.,C de G., COMMANDING
2/7th. BN. DUKE OF WELLINGTON'S REGIMENT.

IN THE FIELD.   MONDAY.   29th. OCTOBER 1917

1. The Battalion will march to the GOMMIECOURT – COURCELLES Area to-morrow, October 30th.
   The march will be resumed on 31st. October to the COUY – SIMENCOURT Area.

2. The starting point will be the Y.M.C.A. at Road Junction BEAULENCOURT. Head of the Column will pass the starting Point at 7.30 a.m.

3. ORDER OF MARCH :- 'A' Coy, 'B' Coy, 'C' Coy, 'D' Coy, Headquarters will parade with their respective Companies. Intervals of 100 yards will be maintained between Coys.

4. Transport (Including Baggage Wagons) will accompany the Battalion.
   Interval of 100 yards will be maintained between near Company and Transport.

5. Reveille to-morrow will be at 5.0 a.m.
   Breakfast at 5.30 a.m.
   Parade. Companies will march on Markers at 7.0 a.m.
   Dress :- Marching Order, with Steel Helmets.
   Watches will be synchronised at Battalion Headquarters at 7.30 p.m. this evening.

6. All Blankets, Jerkins, Coy Stores, Mess Kits, Boxes, Valises etc. will be stacked at the Q.M.Stores at 6 a.m. to-morrow.

7. Lieut. H.L. Hopper and 10 O.R. from 'A' Coy will remain behind to hand over Camp. He will obtain Certificate of cleanliness of Camp and Receipts for Tentage and Stores from the Area Commandant before leaving. He will hand a duplicate of the Certificate and Receipts to Bn. Orderly Room after arrival at GOUY.

8. The Regulations laid down in Section 2 of 62nd. Divisional War Standing Orders will be carefully observed.
   The Return mentioned in Section 2, Para. 7 of those Orders, will be rendered to Battalion Orderly Room as soon as possible after arrival to-morrow.
   O.C.Companies will take steps to ensure that no man falls out on this march.

                        (Sgd) W.C.POGSON, Lieut. & A/Adjt.,
                        2/7th. Bn. Duke of Wellington's Regiment.

APPENDIX 5.

BATTALION ORDER
by
LIEUT. COLONEL F.G. CHAMBERLIN, M.C., C de G. COMMANDING
2/7th. BN. DUKE OF WELLINGTON'S REGIMENT.

IN THE FIELD.   TUESDAY.   30th. OCTOBER 1917.

1. The Battalion will march to the Area GOUY - SIMENCOURT to-morrow 31st. October.

2. The Starting Point will be the Road Junction immediately East of last 'E' in COURCELLES LE COMTE. Head of the Column will pass the Starting Point at 8.45 a.m.

3. Order of March :- 'A' Coy, 'B' Coy, 'C' Coy, 'D' Coy.
Headquarters will parade with their respective Companies.
Intervals will be maintained as to-day.

4. Transport (including Baggage Wagons) will accompany the Battalion.
Interval of 100 yards will be maintained between Rear Company and Transport.

5. Reveille to-morrow will be at 5.30 a.m.
Breakfast at 6.30 a.m.
Parade :- Companies will march on Markers, on Battalion Parade Ground, at 8.0 a.m.
Dress :- Marching Order, with Steel Helmets.
Watches will be synchronised at Battalion Headquarters at 7.45 a.m. to-morrow.

6. All Blankets, Jerkins, Coy Stores, Mess Kits, Boxes, Valises, etc. will be stacked at the Quartermaster's Stores not later than 7.0 a.m.
Blankets will be rolled tightly in bundles of 10 and properly labelled.
A proportionate number of Jerkins will be rolled in each bundle of blankets.
The above Order will be strictly complied with.

7. O.C.Companies will take steps to ensure that their Company Lines are left in a clean condition.

8. 2/Lieut. G. Hattersley and 10 O.R. will remain behind to hand over the Camp. He will obtain Certificate of cleanliness of Camp from the Area Commandant before leaving. He will hand a duplicate of the Certificate to Battalion Orderly Room after arrival at GOUY.

9. The Regulations laid down in Section 2 of 62nd. Divisional War Standing Orders will be carefully observed.
The Returns mentioned in Section 2, Para. 7. of those Orders will be rendered to Battalion Orderly Room as soon as possible after arrival to-morrow.
O.C.Companies will take steps to ensure that no man falls out on this march.

(Sgd) W.C.POGSON, Lieut. & A/Adjt.,
2/7th. Bn. Duke of Wellington's Regiment.

2/4th Bn. Duke of Wellington's Regt.

Secret

WAR DIARY

in accordance with F.S. Regs.

From:- 1st November 1914
To:- 30th November 1914.

Volume XII

Army Form C. 2118.

WAR DIARY
or
INTELLIGENCE SUMMARY.

1/7 Batty H.Q. Rgt

Place	Date	Hour	Summary of Events and Information	Remarks and references to Appendices
GUOY-EN-ARTOIS (O19a)	1/11/17		FINE. Battalion settling in new billets & clearing up. Lt E.TANNER. M.C. appointed Routing officer.	B.
—	2.11.17		FINE. Inspection of battalion at 10.0 am by C.O. Route march for all companies	B.
—	3.11.17		FINE. Coy route march. Specialists training. Afternoon recreational training	B.
—	4.11.17		FINE. Church Parade & bathing. 2/Lt L.B.SMITH to IV CORPS School for course.	B.
—	5.11.17		FINE. Battalion route march. Men marched very well. 1 NCO man falls out. 2/Lt H.HARRIS is transferred to letter 'B' Coy.	B.
—	6.11.17		FINE. General training. Officers & Platoon Sergts. go to WAILLY to see a Tank demonstration. Lt Col F.G.CHAMBERLIN M.C. O.C. 9 Vacates command of the battalion. Lt T.H.CHAMBERS returns to duty from course. 2/Lt C.SAXTON struck off duty. is posted to letter 'B' Coy.	B.
—	7.11.17		WET. The Battalion proceeds to WAILLY in motor lorries to take part in a Tank demonstration	B.
—	8.11.17		FINE. Lt Col F.S.THACKERAY. D.S.O. Me reports for duty assumes command of this unit.	B.
—	9.11.17		WET. Major A G.P.FRYERMAN reports for duty as 2nd in command. 2/Lt H.W.SMITH to Course.	B.
—	10.11.17		FINE. 2/Lts A.H.LOCKWOOD & H.I.TROWSDALE report for duty & are posted to 'D' Coy	B.
—	11.11.17		FINE. Church parade. 2/Lt T.S.CLAPHAM returns from leave.	B.

Army Form C. 2118.

WAR DIARY
or
INTELLIGENCE SUMMARY.
(Erase heading not required.)

Instructions regarding War Diaries and Intelligence Summaries are contained in F.S. Regs., Part II. and the Staff Manual respectively. Title pages will be prepared in manuscript.

Place	Date	Hour	Summary of Events and Information	Remarks and references to Appendices
GOUY.en.ARTOIS	12/11/17		Fine. Inspection of Battalion (less C.Coy.) by new G.O.C. Brig. Genl. R.B. BRADFORD V.C.M.C.B.	
"	13/11/17		Fine. Battalion paraded at 6.30pm for march to ACHIET-le-PETIT. Arrive in Camp. B	
"		At 12.30 am. after making a good march. Poor Camp.		
ACHIET.le.PETIT	14/11/17		Fine. Battalion cleaning up in morning. Sports in afternoon.	B
(HENHAM CAMP)	15/11/17		Fine. Parades under Coy arrangements. Football in afternoon.	B
"	16/11/17		Fine. Battalion moved off 7.15pm. Arrive at Railway Near Camp. LECHELLE at	B
		1.45am. Battalion marches very well. No falling out.		
LECHELLE (P32.a.4.1)	17/11/17		Fine. Battalion resting. Lt. N.T. LAWTON joins for duty	B
LECHELLE	18/11/17		Fine. Battalion moves off at 4.10p.m. Arrive at BERTINCOURT 8.45 p.m. No fallingout	B
BERTINCOURT	19/11/17		Fine. Battalion prepare for the attack (Ammunition bombs etc drawn to each)	B
Line	20/11/17		Fine. Operations in accordance with Appendix 1	Appendix 1
"	21/11/17		Fine. Operations in accordance with Appendix 1	B " " 1
"	22/11/17		Fine. Operations in accordance with Appendix 1	B " " 1
HAVRINCOURT WOOD	23/11/17		Fine. Battalion moves into billets at BERTINCOURT. arriving 1am. General cleaning up	B
BERTINCOURT	24/11/17		Fine. Battalion cleaning up in morning (Ammunition bombs etc drawn ready for moving	B
		up the line)		

WAR DIARY
INTELLIGENCE SUMMARY

Army Form C. 2118.

2/7 S/m Rgt

Place	Date	Hour	Summary of Events and Information	Remarks and references to Appendices
BERTINCOURT	25.11.17		Line Battalion gets ready to proceed to the line in accordance with Appendix 2	Appendix 2 &
LINE	26.11.17		Wet. Operation in accordance with Appendix 2	— " — &
— " —	27.11.17		Wet. Operation in accordance with Appendix 2	— " — &
— " —	28.11.17		Fine. Operation in accordance with Appendix 2	— " — &
— " —	29.11.17		Fine. Operation in accordance with Appendix 2	— " — &
— " —	30.11.17		Fine. Operation in accordance with Appendix 2	— " — &

F. S. Thackeray
Lt. Col.
Commanding 2/7th Batt. of Welsh glm Regt.

APPENDIX. I

2/7th Bn. Duke of Wellington's Regiment.

NARRATIVE of ATTACKS

on 20th and 21st November 1917.

At 5.50 a.m. the Battalion left BERTINCOURT arriving at assembly point HAVRINCOURT WOOD at 7.55 a.m. and leaving at 10 a.m. We moved off in fours behind the 2/4th Bn. along Shropshire Spur Road through FEMY WOOD, then in artillery formation via T. WOOD, Chapel Wood, crossing the Blue Line about K.22.d.6.0. to junction of Sunken Roads at K.16.d. along Road running North East then Northwards along back of HINDENBURG LINE until we came upon the 2/6th Bn. held up about K.10.d.8.5. Here we waited for some time when the Brigadier came up and ordered us to pass through the 2/6th Bn. This we did, and pushed on quickly in artillery formation:-   "A"   "B", the 2/4th Battn.
                                   "C"   "D"

moving forward slightly behind us on our right.   At about K.10.b.6.3. we came upon three abandoned guns (77mm) and then came under fire from two more about K.4.d.6.0. but "D" Coy pushed on and with the help of a Tank captured these and 1 Officer and 15 men. "A" Coy after severe fighting and capturing one machine gun, consolidated the Sunken Road and "B" Coy pushed on to their objective after clearing a block and capturing five machine guns. "C" Coy, who had been helping "B" Coy and "D" Coy then bombed their way on to their final objectives but were delayed for some time by a block and by a shortage of bombs. There were a great number of dugouts in this part of the trench in E.28.b. and E.22.d. and these took some time to mop up and this was not completed until about 10 p.m.
"C" and "D" Coys were placed under command of Lieut. Stott. "C" Coy then were in touch with the 2/5th Bn. at E.22.c.8.0. and held the trench from that point to E.22.d.4.5. with outposts in front and support Platoon in front line of HINDENBURG SUPPORT.
"D" Coy held the line from E.22.d.4.5. to CAMBRAI ROAD E.28.b.7.5.
"B" Coy held the line from E.28.b.4.4. to Sunken Road at E.28.d.4.4.
Touch was obtained with 2/4th Duke of Wellington's Regt by patrols.
"A" Coy consolidated the Sunken Road from E.28.d.0.5. to E.29.c.1.0 and had a Vickers gun guarding either flank.
The night of 20/21st was extremely quiet.
Early next morning orders were received to take part in a Brigade attack with Tanks on BOURLON VILLAGE, BOURLON WOOD and ANNEUX. The objective allotted to the Battalion being the trenches running from E.24.b.8.5. to the CRUCIFIX E.17.a.7.9. The attack was ordered to commence at 10 a.m. and at that hour the Battalion moved forward from its forming up line in the Sunken Road running N.W. and S.E. through the Factory. "A" Coy. on right, "D" Coy in centre, and "C" on the left, "B" Coy being in support. Progress was made very quickly although the Tanks did not arrive up to time, but just before reaching the Sunken Road running through E.24.a. and b. came under heavy machine gun fire from the trench and the wood but managed to reach the road at about E.24.c.9.9. capturing on the way two 5.9 howitzers. Further progress from this point was impossible on account of the uncut wire which was very thick. The Tanks eventually turned up but by this time

(1)

the enemy were thoroughly ready for us and although many
attempts to get forward were made and some progress was
made in places, these were only temporary advantages.
The advance of "A" "D" and "C" Coys was so rapid that a
gap was formed between "C" Company and the 2/5th Bn. who
were unable to make such quick progress in their oblique
attack on the Road from the CRUCIFIX to E.15.d. central.
To fill this it became necessary to throw in "B" Coy and
to ask for the help of two Coys of the 2/5th Battn. This
was given and proved invaluable as the enemy appeared
likely to make a counter attack from this flank. The
Battalion held on to this position until relieved about
6 p.m. by the 2/8th West Yorkshire Regiment. The Battn
then moved back to the vicinity of the Sunken Road in E.28.d.
when it stayed the night of the 21/22nd and until 9 p.m.
on the 22nd when it marched to shacks in Havrincourt
Wood which it reached at 4 a.m. The following is a list
of casualties which were very light and nearly all machine
gun bullet wounds:-

Capt. Gloag.M.C.   Wounded.
Capt. Alexander.M.C.   "
Lieut. Stott.   "
Lieut. Maden.   "
2/Lieut. Crockson.   "
2/Lieut. Lockwood.   Shell Shock.

    4 O.R. killed.
   59 O.R. wounded.

BOURLON VILLAGE

1:5,000

Scale — 1:5,000

The information concerning roads and banks is taken from refugees' statements.

BOURLON.

SECRET.

War diary APPENDIX 2

2/7th Bn. DUKE of WELLINGTON'S REGIMENT.

Narrative of Events from 25th
November to night 3/4th Dec. 1917.

The 186th Brigade moved off on Sunday 25th November at 1.30 p.m. to take over the trenches in BOURLON WOOD from the 2nd Scots Guards and elements of 119th Brigade.

The 2/7th Duke of Wellington's Regt. took over the line roughly along road from F.14.a.5.3. to F.7.d.3.4. from the 2nd Scots Guards and the 2/6th Duke of Wellington's Regiment took over a line running roughly along road F.7.d.3.4. to F.13.a.1.8. etc from 119th Brigade, the 2/4th and 2/5th Duke of Wellington's being in support.

The line taken over by the Battalion from the Scots Guards consisted of unconnected posts close up to the top of the ridge.

The Battalion was disposed as follows:-
"D" Company on right, "B" in centre and "A" on left. "C" Company had one Platoon in a strong point about F.13.b.5.5. and two Platoons were in support near Battalion Headquarters at the CHALET about F.13.d.1.9. the highest point being in NO MAN'S LAND. The enemy were very active with machine guns and sniping.

The 26th November was spent on consolidating our positions. On the night of the 26th orders were given for an attack on BOURLON VILLAGE the next morning, the objective given to the Battalion being the area bounded by the railway line from F.1.d.2.1. to the road crossing F.1.6.3.7. on the North, the road running from F.7.a.0.9. to F.1.c.3.7. on the West, and on the South the road running from F.7.a.0.9. to F.7.b.2.4. (exclusive of houses on the North side of this road).

Prior to the attack an alteration of disposition was arranged:- The 2/5th relieved the Battalion in the front line and the Battalion moved into support about F.13.c.

At 6.20 (zero hour) 27th November, the Battalion moved forward from it's forming-up line on the road F.13.b.2.5. to F.13.a.4.8. behind the 2/6th Duke of Wellington's Regiment. The 2/6th D. of W's were however very soon held up by machine gun fire and the Battalion pushed on through them until it eventually got to a position about F.7.a. central and to the S.E. of this two Companies, "C" and "D", getting to the FACTORY at F.7.b.0.3. and two Companies, "A" and "B", to the FACTORY at F.7.a.6.6.; they were then well in front of our troops on the right (2/7th West Yorks) and there appeared to be no one on the left. Captain Miller, who was in command of "A" Company, as he was unable to get forward any further owing to heavy machine gun fire from the Railway Cutting, determined to refuse his left flank which was in the air and ordered "C" Company to take up a position as shown on map.

At 3.45 p.m. the Germans counter-attacked from the West and North and at the same time the 2/7th West Yorks were driven back on our right. As there appeared to be little chance of our holding these positions which were in a very thick part of the wood, the order was given to

(1)

withdraw gradually to the old German line which was well forward of our original line and gave a good field of fire and good observation.

That night the line was taken over by the 4th Cavalry Battalion and the Battalion moved back into support in F.13.a. and stayed there until relieved the next night (28th) by the 18th London Regiment.

The Battalion then moved to trenches in K.3.d. where it stayed until the evening of the 30th when the Brigade was ordered to concentrate and the Battalion was ordered to move to K.9.d. The Battalion stayed here one night and was then amalgamated into two Companies, "A" and "D" No. 1 Coy, "B" and "C" No. 2 Company, and on the evening of the 1st December was ordered to support the 6th Brigade and took over trenches vacated by 22nd R.F. as follows:-

No. 1 Coy. E.26.d.7.3. to E.26.d.1.8. with supporting Platoon in trench E.26.d.3.2. to E.26.d.1.8.
No. 2 Coy. E.26.c.9.6. to E.25.b.5.5.
Battalion Headquarters E.26.d.8.0.

The Battalion stayed in these positions, where it suffered some casualties, until relieved by 11th Argyll & Sutherland Highlanders on the night of 3/4th December when it marched to VELU.

Casualties:-

2/Lieut. J.S.Quarmby. Killed.
2/Lieut. G.A.Cartwright. Wounded - died of wounds.

42 other ranks Killed.
143 " " wounded.
4 " " wounded and missing.
2 " " wounded & missing, believed killed.
1 " " died of wounds.
2 " " shell shock.
9 " " Missing.

2/Lieut. C. Sexton. Wounded. 27.11.17.
2/Lieut. A.V.Spafford. Wounded. 27.11.17.
2/Lieut. H.Hartley. Wounded. 27.11.17.
Lieut. N.T.Lawton. Wounded. 27.11.17.

Lieut. Colonel,
Commanding,
2/7th Bn.Duke of Wellington's Regt.

2/7th Bn. Duke of Wellington's (W.R) Regiment.

ORIGINAL

SECRET.

WAR DIARY

rendered in accordance with F.S. Regulations

From:- 1st December 1914.
To:- 31st December 1914.

Volume 12.

E. S. Thaleny........ Lt. Colonel
Commanding.
2/7th BN. DUKE OF WELLINGTON'S REGT.

Original

WAR DIARY
or
INTELLIGENCE SUMMARY.
(Erase heading not required.)

1/6 Bn Duke of Wellingtons Regt.

Army Form C. 2118.

Place	Date	Hour	Summary of Events and Information	Remarks and references to Appendices
LINE	1/12/17		Fine. Operation in accordance with Appendix 2	See Appendix 2
" "	2/12/17		Fine. Operation in accordance with Appendix 2	do " "
" "	3/12/17		Fine. Operation in accordance with Appendix 2	do " "
" "	4/12/17		Orders received that the 1/6 Bn Duke of Wellington's were to relieve the Battalion moving by Companies into camp at LABUQUIERE during the am	do
LABUQUIERE	4/12/17		Fine. Battalion moved off at 11 am to entrain at FREMICOURT. Detrained at BEAUMETZ & marched into billets at BAILLEUVAL. Orders received to move next days to GOUBES	do
BAILLEUVAL	5/12/17		Fine. Battalion moved off for GOUBES at 2 pm arriving 5 pm. Good march. Battalion located in three huts. Orders received to move next day to TINQUES.	do
GOUBES	6/12/17		Fine. Battalion marched to TINQUES arriving 11 am. Located in billets & barns.	do
TINQUES	7/12/17		Fine. General cleaning up & inspections. No training	do
" "	8/12/17		Fine. Battalion located at Divisional rest. No training. The 1/6 Inniskillings inoculated to England for transfer to the Indian Army	do
" "	9/12/17		Fine. Church parade in the morning. Inspection of Companies by O/C in the afternoon	do

Army Form C. 2118.

Original 2/7 Bn Duke of Wellington Regt

WAR DIARY
or
INTELLIGENCE SUMMARY.
(Erase heading not required.)

Instructions regarding War Diaries and Intelligence Summaries are contained in F.S. Regs., Part II. and the Staff Manual respectively. Title pages will be prepared in manuscript.

Place	Date	Hour	Summary of Events and Information	Remarks and references to Appendices
TINQUES	9.12.17	(cont.)	Lt. S.P. Heyward proceeded on leave. Orders received for move to LAPUGNOY.	—
TINQUES	10.12.17	Fine	Battalion marched to LAPUGNOY. Good march. One fell out. Battalion billeted in huts.	—
LAPUGNOY	11.12.17	WET	General regimental routine. 2/Lt. A.B. Smith returned from course.	—
" "	12.12.17	FINE	General regimental routine. Companies reorganised into two Platoons.	—
" "	13.12.17	Fine	Battalion on the range. Inspection of Transport by new G.O.C. Brig Genl Burnett. Orders received for move to BUSNETTES.	—
" "	14.12.17	Wet	Battalion marched to BUSNETTES. Moved at 10.40 a.m. Arrive 12.20 p.m. No falling out.	—
BUSNETTES	15.12.17	Fine	General regimental routine in the morning. Paper chase in the afternoon. 2/Lt J. Buckley returned from course.	—
" "	16.12.17	Cold little snow	No church parade. 2/Lt Red Smith returned from course.	—
" "	17.12.17	Very cold & snowing	Battalion wrote march 2/9. Orders received to march to LAPUGNOY.	—
" "	18.12.17	Fine	Battalion marched to LAPUGNOY. Orders received to move the following day to TINQUES. No falling out.	—

Army Form C. 2118.

WAR DIARY
or
INTELLIGENCE SUMMARY

(Erase heading not required.)

Original

2/7th DUKE OF WELLINGTONS REGT

Place	Date	Hour	Summary of Events and Information	Remarks and references to Appendices
LAPUGNOY	19/10/17		The Battalion marched to TINQUES. No falling out feates in Billet 2:30 p.m.	J.S.
TINQUES	"		The following decorations were received from IV Corps for gallantry during the operation which commenced on 20th November 1917. MILITARY MEDAL 306861 Pte Crowther F. 8539 Pte Smith R.305852 Cpl Koch G. 11826 Pte Healey E. 28041 Pte Tunstill J. 305946 Pte Argyle M. 30588 L/Cpl Allen J. 30690 G. Pte Bayron B. 306831 Pte Gracow J.M. 115005 L/Cpl Robinson B. 16300 Pte Crowther A. 306155 Sgt Cooper W 305369 Sgt Roberg A. 17875 Pte Kenworthy H. 305219 Pte Holder J. 306701 Pte Ewell H. 305-152 Sgt Hitchfoot A 306625 Pte Thornbury J. 85140 Pte Taylor J. 9154 Pte Baylis J. 305944 Pte Cyrus J. BAR TO MILITARY MEDAL 7302 L/Cpl Woolley R. Authority D.R.O. 1049 dated 18/10/17. General Regimental routine. Training under specialist officers. Lieut Sidney Noble reported for duty was posted to "B" Company.	J.S. J.S.
TINQUES	20/10/17		General Regimental Routine. Training under specialist officers. The Battalion area. Lieut J.S. Clapham proceeded to GRANTHAM to join M.G. Corps.	J.S. J.S.

Original

Army Form C. 2118.

WAR DIARY
or
INTELLIGENCE SUMMARY.
(Erase heading not required.)

Instructions regarding War Diaries and Intelligence Summaries are contained in F. S. Regs., Part II. and the Staff Manual respectively. Title pages will be prepared in manuscript.

2/7th DUKE OF WELLINGTON'S REGT

Place	Date	Hour	Summary of Events and Information	Remarks and references to Appendices
TINQUES	21/12/17		General Regimental Routine. Lt W.A. Awdell proceeded to LA BRAYELLE to be posted in "Battalion of Canadiens" by Col Sir Ian Alexander King.	
TINQUES	23/12/17		Intensely cold. Freezing all day. Church Parade in the morning.	F.S.G.
TINQUES	24/12/17		General Regimental Routine. A & C Companies found the usual working parties.	F.S.G.
TINQUES	25/12/17		Warmer owing to thaw. Captain G.W.W. Miller proceeded on leave. Weather very cold, snowing heavily. Church Parade in the morning. Xmas Christmas dinner at mid-day.	F.S.G.
TINQUES	26/12/17		Much snow. Very cold. General Regimental Routine.	F.S.G.
TINQUES	27/12/17		Much less very cold. B & D Companies fired on range. C & D Companies firing. Lewis gunners fired under Test Ft Attilery. Remainder of C & D practised wiring.	F.S.Q.
TINQUES	28/12/17		Weather cold. B & D Company fired on range. A & C Companies musketry. Bombers. Musketry Lewis Gun officer. Companies inspected by Divisional Gas officer in afternoon.	F.S.Q.
TINQUES	29/12/17		Snow. General Regimental Routine. 2/Lt P Haywood & 2/Lt E Townsend & 2/Lt A Collins & 1/Lt Brush proceeded	F.S.Q.

Original

WAR DIARY
or
INTELLIGENCE SUMMARY.
(Erase heading not required.)

Army Form C. 2118.

2/7th Duke of Wellingtons Regt

Place	Date	Hour	Summary of Events and Information	Remarks and references to Appendices
TINQUES	30/12/17		Church Parade in the morning	
TINQUES	31/12/17		C.O. + 1 officer per company provided up the line to reconnoitre area, all entrenches practice "company in the attack". The following awards for gallantry during operations which commenced on 30th November 1917 were received this day. The Military Cross Lieut S.P. Hayward & Lieut T.G.W. Pepper (Authority D.R.O 1083 dated 30/12/(17) The Distinguished Conduct Medal 305515 Sgt Robinson B (Authority D.R.O 1083 dated 30/12/17.	328. 325.

F.S. Shelmer
Lt. Colonel
Commanding.
2/7th BN. DUKE OF WELLINGTON'S REGT.

APPENDIX 2.

2/7th Bn. DUKE of WELLINGTON'S REGIMENT.

NARRATIVE OF EVENTS FROM 25th

NOVEMBER TO NIGHT 3/4th DECEMBER 1917.

The 186th Brigade moved off on Sunday 25th November at 1.30 p.m. to take over the trenches in BOURLON WOOD from the 2nd Scots Guards and elements of 119th Brigade.

The 2/7th Bn. took over the line roughly along road from F.14.a.5.3. to F.7.d.2.4. from the 2nd Scots Guards and the 2/6th Duke of Wellington's Regiment took over a line running roughly along road F.7.d.3.4. to F.13.a.1.8 etc from 119th Brigade.

The 2/4th and 2/5th Duke of Wellington's Regiment were in support.

The line taken over by the Battalion from the Scots Guards consisted of unconnected posts close up to the top of the ridge. The Battalion was disposed as follows:-
"D" Coy on right. "B" in centre and "A" on the left.
"C" Coy had one platoon in a strong point about F.13.b.5.5. and two platoons were in support near Battalion Headquarters at The Chalet about F.13.d.1.9.

The highest points were in No Man's Land. The enemy were very active with machine guns and sniping.

The 26th November was spent in consolidating our positions. On the night of the 26th orders were given for an attack on BOURLON VILLAGE the next morning, the objective given to the Battalion being the area bounded by the railway line from F.1.d.2.1. to the road crossing F.1.c.3.7. on the North, the road running from F.7.a.0.9 to F.1.c.3.7. on the West and on the South the road running from F.7.a.0.9 to F.7.b.2.4. (exclusive of houses on the North side of this road.)

Prior to the attack, an alteration of disposition was arranged; the 2/5th relieved the Battalion in the front line and the Battalion moved into support about F.13.c.

At 6.20 (zero hour) 27th November, the Battalion moved forward from it's forming-up line on the road F.13.b.2.5. to F.13.a.4.8. behind the 2/6th Duke of Wellington's Regt. The 2/6th were however very soon held up by machine gun fire and the Battalion pushed on through them until it eventually got to a position about F.7.a.central and to the South East of this, two Companies "C" and "D" getting to the Factory at F.7.b.0.3. and two Companies "A" and "B" to the Factory at F.7.a.6.6. They were then well in front of our troops on the right (2/5th West Yorks) and there appeared to be no one on the left. Capt. Miller, who was in command of "A" Coy, as he was unable to get forward any further owing to heavy machine gun fire from the railway cutting, determined to refix his left flank which was in the air and ordered "C" Coy to take up a position as shown on map.

At 3.45 p.m. the Germans counter-attacked from the West and North and at the same time the 2/5th West Yorks were driven back on our right. As there appeared to be little chance of our holding these positions which were in a very thick part of the Wood, the order was given to withdraw gradually to the old German line which was well forward of our original line and gave a good field of fire and good observation.

That night the line was taken over by the 4th Cavalry

Battalion and the Battalion moved back into support in F.13.a. and stayed there until relieved the next night (28th) by the 18th London Regiment.

The Battalion then moved to trenches in K.3.d. where it stayed until the evening of the 30th when the Brigade was ordered to concentrate and the Battalion was ordered to K.9.d. The Battalion stayed here one night and was then amalgamated into two Companies, "A" and "D" No. 1 Company, "C"/ and "B" No. 2 Company, and ion the evening of the 1st December was ordered up to support the 6th Brigade and took over trenches evacuated by 22nd R.F8s as follows:-

No. 1 Company:- E.26.d.7.3. to E.26.d.1.8 with supporting
Platoon in trench E.26.d.3.2. to E.26.d.1.8.
No. 2 Company:- E.26.c.9.6. to E.25.b.5.5.
Battalion Headquarters E.26.d.8.0.

The Battalion stayed in these positions where it suffered some casualties until relieved by 11th Argyll and Sutherland Highlanders on the night of 3/4th December when it marched to VELUX.

Casualties:-

2/Lieut. J.S.Quarmby.	Killed.
2/Lieut. G.A.Cartwright.	Wounded - died of wounds.
2/Lieut. C. Sexton.	Wounded.
2/Lieut. A.V.Spafford.	Wounded.
2/Lieut. H.Hartley.	"
Lieut. N.T.Lawton.	"

42	other	ranks	killed.
141	"	"	wounded.
3	"	"	wounded and missing.
2	"	"	shell shock.
9	"	"	missing.
1	"	"	reported killed.
2	"	"	wounded & missing, believed killed.
1	"	"	died of wounds.
1	"	"	wounded, believed killed.

Lieut. Colonel,
Commanding,
2/7th Bn. Duke of Wellington's Regiment.

Vol. 13

18/62

War Diary

of

H.Q. R.E. of Pethinglands Bgl.

From January 1st 1918 to January 21st 1915

Volume 13.

13 #

13 cheats

F. S. Dudban Lieut. Colonel
O.C. H.Q. R.E. of Pethingland 1916.

Army Form C. 2118.

Original

WAR DIARY
or
INTELLIGENCE SUMMARY.
(Erase heading not required.)

Instructions regarding War Diaries and Intelligence Summaries are contained in F.S. Regs., Part II. and the Staff Manual respectively. Title pages will be prepared in manuscript.

2/7TH DUKE OF WELLINGTONS REGT

Place	Date	Hour	Summary of Events and Information	Remarks and references to Appendices
TINQUES	1/1/18		"A"+"B" companies firing on range. "C"+"D" companies. Artillery formation and Company in the attack.	w.g.
TINQUES	2/1/18		All companies passed through gas chamber at CHELERS for testing of respirators. Field Gr HATTERSLEY witnessed troops line demonstration. General Regimental Routine.	w.g.
TINQUES	3/1/18		All companies found on parade 2 platoons on picket from A+B Coys in the attack	w.g.
TINQUES	4/1/17		G.O.C. inspected battalion & presented medal ribbons to recipients of military Crosses, Distinguished Conduct Medal, and Military medal as above (vide 19/9/17 & 31/12/17)	w.g.
TINQUES	5/1/17		"A"+"B" Companies firing in morning "C"+"D" companies firing in afternoon. Lt Gr HATTERSLEY proceeded on leave.	w.g.
TINQUES	6/1/17		Church Parade in the morning. Instruction	w.g.
TINQUES	7/1/17		morning Scheme "Battalion in advance guard" afternoon C+D companies firing	w.g.
TINQUES	8/1/17		Ordinary Regimental Routine. Instructions. War Diary and onions	w.g.
TINQUES	9/1/18		Snow the ... entrained at MAROEUIL arrived the ...	w.g.

Army Form C. 2118.

Original

WAR DIARY
or
INTELLIGENCE SUMMARY.
(Erase heading not required.)

2/4th Duke of Wellington's Regt

Instructions regarding War Diaries and Intelligence Summaries are contained in F.S. Regs., Part II. and the Staff Manual respectively. Title pages will be prepared in manuscript.

Place	Date	Hour	Summary of Events and Information	Remarks and references to Appendices
MAROEUIL	10/1/18		Change in weather, 3 officers (West Yorks Regt) reported for duty	1004.
MAROEUIL	11/1/18		Ordinary Regimental Routine.	1004.
MAROEUIL	12/1/18		Line. Ordinary Regimental Routine.	1004.
MAROEUIL	13/1/18		Church Parades. Ordinary Regimental Routine.	1004.
MAROEUIL	14/1/18		Battalion relieved 2/4th York Rancers Regiment in the line in accordance with appendix 3.	3 1007.
IN THE LINE	15/1/18		Battalion in the line in accordance with appendix 3	3 1004.
IN THE LINE	16/1/18		Weather very wet in the line (appendix 3)	3 1004.
IN THE LINE	17/1/18		Very deep mud in the trenches, in the line (appendix 3)	3 1007.
IN THE LINE	18/1/18		Battalion came out into brigade reserve area (See Appendix 4)	4 1004.
WAKEFIELD CAMP.	19/1/18		Two companies at WAKEFIELD CAMP, two companies at CHANTECLER	1004.
WAKEFIELD CAMP.	20/1/18		Ordinary Regimental Routine.	1004.
WAKEFIELD CAMP.	21/1/18		Ordinary Regimental Routine.	1004.
WAKEFIELD CAMP.	22/1/18		Battalion moved into the RED LINE (See appendix 5)	5 1004.

D. D. & L., London, E.C. Wt W17771/M2031 750,000 5/17 Sch. 53 Forms/C2118/14 (A8cq4)

Army Form C. 2118.

Original

WAR DIARY
or
INTELLIGENCE SUMMARY
(Erase heading not required.)

2/4th Duke of Wellington's Regt

Instructions regarding War Diaries and Intelligence Summaries are contained in F.S. Regs., Part II. and the Staff Manual respectively. Title pages will be prepared in manuscript.

Place	Date	Hour	Summary of Events and Information	Remarks and references to Appendices
In the Line	23/1/16		Battalion in RED LINE.	scrap
IN THE LINE	24/1/16		Weather fine, working parties.	scrap
IN THE LINE	25/1/16		Fine working parties.	scrap
IN THE LINE	26/1/16		Companies subtly working parties.	scrap
IN THE LINE	27/1/16		Weather fine, working parties.	scrap
IN THE LINE	28/1/16		Working parties.	scrap
IN THE LINE	29/1/16		Working all day.	scrap
IN THE LINE	30/1/16		Battalion moves to WAKEFIELD CAMP in accordance with Appendix b.	6 scrap
WAKEFIELD CAMP	31/1/16		Ordinary Regimental Routine. 12 Officers + 240/55 O.R. posted to this Battalion from 2/6th Bn. D. of W. Regiment on the disbanding of that battalion.	scrap

J. S. Thelwars
Lieutenant Colonel
Comdg
2/4th Duke of Wellington's Regt.

War Diary
Appendix 3

OPERATION ORDERS
by
LIEUT. COLONEL F.S. THACKERAY D.S.O., M.C. COMMANDING
2/7th Bn. Duke of Wellington's Regiment.

IN THE FIELD.   SATURDAY.   JANUARY 12th 1918.
....

1. The Battalion will relieve the 2/4th Bn. York & Lancs Regiment in the left sub-section of the Brigade Front on the 14th inst. The Battalion will proceed by train leaving MAROEUIL in time to arrive at CHANTICLER SIDING at 9.0 a.m.

2. An advance party, as under, will proceed up the line to-morrow, Sunday. Unless further orders are issued, this party will parade at Battalion Headquarters at 8.0 a.m. tomorrow prompt, and will march off under the senior Officer.
    1 Officer per Company.
    1 N.C.O. per Platoon.
    1 other rank for each Lewis Gun Team.
    Lieut. Tanner from H.Q. with two runners and a signaller.
Guides from 187th Bde will meet them at CHANTICLER SIDING AT 10. a.m.

3. All troops must enter the trenches at the Eastern entrance of TOBY ALLEY.
Stretchers and Lewis Guns must not be carried on the shoulder when moving in the trenches.

4. All Defence Schemes, trench maps and photographs will be taken over and also all details for work in hand and proposed work. Lists of ammunition and trench Stores will be forwarded to Battalion Headquarters as early as possible.

5. "A" and "B" Coys will occupy the front line.
Half of "D" Coy will be attached to "A" Coy for duty, the other half being in CECIL SUPPORT.
"D" Coy's Headquarters will be at the Headquarters of "A" Coy.

One half of "C" Coy will be in RAILWAY TRENCH and the other half at Battalion Headquarters at MARINE TRENCH.

6. Personnel of Battalion Headquarters will be prepared to man a defensive position if occasion demands.

7. During the tour in the line, Companies will be allotted a four hours task by day and night instead of the usual time table being issued for work.

8. The foot-rubbing return will be due at 12 noon.

9. Dress:- Fighting Order. Leather Jerkins will be worn.

10. The Transport Officer will arrange to bring to Battalion Headquarters to-morrow Sunday, Lewis Gun Magazines required for the line. The number of these will be notified to him by the Battalion Lewis Gun N.C.O.

11. Blankets, (in bundles of 10), men's packs, and all stores, valises etc required to be taken to the transport lines, will be stacked at Battalion Headquarters not later than 8.0 a.m. on the 14th inst.

/Sgd/ H. ORMEROD. Captain & Adjutant.
2/7th Bn. Duke of Wellington's Regt.

War Diary Appendix 3.

AMENDMENT TO OPERATION ORDERS of even date
by
LIEUT. COLONEL F.S.THACKERAY D.S.O., M.C. COMMANDING
2/7th Bn. DUKE OF WELLINGTON'S REGIMENT
IN THE FIELD.   SATURDAY.   JANUARY 12th 1918.
....

                                                                                       (to-morrow)

Ref. Para 2. The advance party will parade at Bn. H.Q. at 7.45 a.m. and move off under the senior officer in time to report to the R.T.O. MAROEUIL by 8.5 a.m.

Lieut. E. Tanner M.C. will detail guides to meet the Battalion where the duckboards begin in Railway Cutting at 9.15 a.m. on the 14th inst.

The Battalion will proceed in the following order on the 14th inst:- "B" Coy. "D" Coy, "A" Coy, "C" Coy.   Should any alteration to this order be necessary, Lieut. Tanner will send word to CHANTECLER SIDING by the senior guide.

Ref. Para.5. Personnel of "D" Coy who are to be attached to "A" Coy will report to O.C. "A" Coy prior to leaving present billets.

                                        /Sgd/ H. ORMEROD. Captain & Adjutant.
                                        2/7th Bn. Duke of Wellington's Regiment.

Operation Orders
by
Lieut. Colonel F.S. Thackeray, D.S.O. M.C.
Commanding
2/7th Bn. Duke of Wellington's Regt.

Thursday.   17.1.18

① The Battalion will be relieved in the line by the 2/6th Bn Duke of Wellington's Regt as under :-
"A" Coy 2/6th Bn. will relieve our "D" Coy
"B"   "   "   "   "   "   "   "C" "
"C"   "   "   "   "   "   "   "A" "
"D"   "   "   "   "   "   "   "B" "

On relief Companies will move to positions as under :-
"A" & "D" to WAKEFIELD CAMP.
"B" & "C" " Billets close to Brigade HQ.

Details of relief will be arranged between Co.C. Companies concerned.

Guides for incoming Unit will rendezvous at Battn HQ at 10.30 am

Guides for Rear Camp will meet this Unit on the main road near Brigade HQ. Quartermaster will arrange.

(2) All Lewis Gun Drums will be handed over and a similar number taken over from the Reserve Battalion by the Quartermaster, with the exception of 4 Guns of "C" Coy and 1 Gun of "B" Coy.

(3) The Quartermaster will take over the Camp by 8 a.m. tomorrow (H.Q. near Brigade).
One man per Company (from Stores) and one man from H.Q. will accompany him and act as guides for the Battalion.

(4) All stores, mess boxes and any surplus stores will be dumped at Battalion Ration Dump by 3 p.m. to be moved by transport as early as possible.
This will include Lewis Guns with the exception of 4 Guns from "C" Coy and 1 Gun from "B" Coy.
1 O.R. per Lewis Gun and 1 h C.O. from H.Q. will remain with these stores.

3.

(5) Transport will take Officers' Valises, mens packs and blankets &c. to the new Camp in time for the Battalion.

(6) A Working Party table will be issued later.

(7) Guides will report to O.C. "C" Coy and O.C. "B" Coy to guide the 4 Guns of "C" and 1 Gun of "B" to their new positions as arranged by them today.

(Sgd) H Ormerod Capt & Adjt
2/7 Duke of Wellington's Regt

[handwritten: Edw Wray] *[handwritten: Attached is 5]*

OPERATION ORDERS
by
LIEUT-COLONEL F.S. THACKERAY, D.S.O., M.C., COMMANDING
2/7TH. BN. DUKE OF WELLINGTON'S REGIMENT.

IN THE FIELD.   MONDAY.   21st. JANUARY 1918.

----

(1) The Battalion will relieve the 2/5th. Bn. York & Lancs Regt. in the RED LINE to-morrow, 22nd. instant.

(2) An Advance Party of 1 Officer and 1 N.C.O. per Company and Lieut. J.E. Charlesworth and 2 runners from Battalion Headquarters will proceed to take over from the 2/5th. Bn. York & Lancs Regt. at 9.0 a.m. from Battalion Headquarters.

(3) Guides from 2/5th. Bn. York & Lancs Regt. will report to Battalion Headquarters at 2.30 p.m. to take up the remainder of the Companies.
Companies will be ready at this place and time.
Dress :- Full Marching Order.

(4) 'C' Company will be on the left and 'B' Coy on the right in the RED LINE in B.25.a. and c.
Headquarters will be in this vicinity.
'A' Coy will be on the left and 'D' Coy on the right in DITCH POST, B.19.b. and B.25.d.

(5) Transport Officer will arrange with O.C. Companies for transport of Lewis Guns in boxes to ration dumps and will notify them where he requires ration parties and the time.

(6) The Quartermaster will ensure that the Limbers reporting to Companies have the requisite numbers of Lewis Gun Magazines, i.e.
'A' Coy. 64., 'B' Coy. 48., 'C' Coy. Nil, 'D' Coy 64.

(7) Limbers will report to Companies and Headquarters for blankets, etc. at 9.30 a.m.
Mess Boxes, etc. will be removed at 2.30 p.m.

(8) All working parties after 9.0 a.m. to-morrow, 22nd. inst. are cancelled.
The following working party will be found by the Battalion to-morrow, 22nd. inst., to rendezvous at Battalion Headquarters at 3.15 p.m. and will proceed under the senior Officer to R.E.d.P.O. (where BRICK LINE CUTS HAVRINCOURT ROAD) :-

'A' Coy. 1 Officer and 40 O.Rks.
'B' "   1   "   " 36   "
'C' "   1   "   " 36   "
'D' "   1   "   " 30   "
         4 Officers and 134 O.Rks.

O.C. 'C' Coy will render parade state to O.C. 'A' Coy of the number of men of the latter's Company who are attached to him and are fit for parade. He will be responsible for their parading.

Dress for above working party :- Full Marching Order.

O.C. Companies will send guides for above working party of their Company to rendezvous, for 'B' and 'C' Coys at Cross Roads

B.22.b.7.0., for 'A' and 'D' Coys at junction of duckboard track and trench at a.4.a.80.65. at 9.30 p.m.

(9) Working Parties after to-morrow, 22nd. inst., will be found as under :-

  <u>Jan. 23rd.</u>   'A' and 'D' Companies will work under R.Es. from 2.0 p.m. to 5.0 p.m. on TONY ALLEY.
   'B' and 'C' Companies will work under R.Es. from 2.0 p.m. to 5.0 p.m. on OUSE ALLEY.

  On January 24th. and subsequent days they will work on the same trenches from 9.0 a.m. to 3.0 p.m.
  This work will be taken over from the 2/5th. Bn. York & Lancs Regt. on relief and care should be taken that the place for report and person to report to are taken over correctly.

(10) All Trench Stores, Trench Maps, Aeroplane Photographs and Defence Schemes will be carefully taken over and Lists of same forwarded to Battalion Headquarters not later than 10.0 a.m. on 23rd. inst. All work in progress and proposed work (in writing and with maps) will be carefully taken over.

(11) Transport Officer will notify Quartermaster number of Petrol Tins required.

(12) Companies will turn out at FULL STRENGTH as work is very urgent.

(13) As the work is day work, O.C.Companies will take steps to prevent men clumping together and will keep them well spread out and as concealed as possible.

(14) Tools will be provided by R.Es.

(15) The object of these working parties is to clear a gangway along the trench, the mud thrown up during by the day working parties will be cleared by the night berm clearing parties already detailed by Brigades.

                    (Sgd) H. GREENROD, Captain & Adjutant,
                         2/7th. Bn. Duke of Wellington's Regiment.

Transport Officer will make necessary arrangements for collection of Water Cart at Right Dump.

Officers' Charges will be at end of duckboard track.

(Sgd) H. ORMEROD, Capt. & Adjt.,
2/7th. Bn. Duke of Wellington's Regiment.

Appendix 6

OPERATION ORDERS
by
LIEUT-COLONEL E.S. ISACKSSAY, D.S.O., M.C., COMMANDING
2/7th. Bn. DUKE OF WELLINGTON'S REGIMENT.

IN THE FIELD.   TUESDAY.   30th. JANUARY 1918.

(1) The Battalion will leave its present billets to-morrow and move to WAKEFIELD CAMP.

(2) Advance Parties report to Lieut. E. Tanner, M.C. at WAKEFIELD CAMP at 8.30 a.m.

(3) All movement will be done by communication trenches.
The route for 'A' and 'D' Companies will be by TOTTY ALLEY, duckboard track, and by road to WAKEFIELD CAMP.
The route for Headquarters, 'B' and 'C' Companies will be, Crossroads E.28.c.7.2., Sunken Road to road junction E.27.b.5.5., thence to Railway Cutting, along Railway Cutting to main road.
(Movement for these latter Companies from trench to Crossroads will be by small parties).
The following distances will be kept:-
   Companies 200 yards.
   Platoons   100   "
Companies will move at following times:-
   'A' Coy.   11.0 a.m.
   'B' "   10.0 a.m.
   'C' "   10.15 a.m.
   'D' "   11.15 a.m.
   H.Q.   10.30 a.m.

(4) All Lewis Guns, spare stores, Ammn Boxes, etc. will be dumped at respective Ration dumps before leaving and a sufficient Guard and loading party left in charge.

Quartermaster will arrange to have blankets, Officers' Valises, etc. at the Camp.

(5) Company Cooks should be sent down immediately after breakfast to prepare dinners for the men.

(6) Lieut. E. Tanner, M.C. will be billeting Officer and will take over the Camp.
He will send guides to meet Companies on the road between CRANTIGNAN and HOULINCOURT.
Lieut. V.A. Hinchcliffe will post runners at the following points to direct parties of men. These runners will join the last party from H.Q. :-
 (1) B.26.b.7.9.   (2) B.27.c.5.6.
 (3) B.27.d.6.3.

(7) It is not yet known, if any, that unit is relieving in the RED LINE. If no advance parties arrive before Companies move off, a senior N.C.O. will be left, with a list of secret documents, which will be handed over to any relieving unit and receipt obtained. If no relief has taken place before the limbers report in the evening, these documents will be handed to Battalion Headquarters at WAKEFIELD CAMP.

(8) The Transport Officer will detail Company Limbers to report at the respective dumps as early as possible in the evening.

(Sgd) J. ORMEROD, Capt., & Adjt.,
2/7th Bn. Duke of Wellington's Regiment.

Vol/14

Secret.

Original

War Diary
~ of ~
2/4th Bn. Duke of Wellington's Regiment

From :- 1st February 1918.
To :- 28th February 1918.

Volume :- XIV.

~~~~~~~

/signature/ Major
commanding
2/4th Bn. Duke of Wellington's Regt.

Original
WAR DIARY
or
INTELLIGENCE SUMMARY.
(Erase heading not required.)

Army Form C. 2118.

2/7th Duke of Wellington's Regt

Place	Date	Hour	Summary of Events and Information	Remarks and references to Appendices
WAREFIELD CAMP	1/8/18		Battalion moved to CHANTICLER as per appendix	App 7 + 8
CHANTICLER	2/8/18		Working parties up the line	App 9
CHANTICLER	3/8/18		Working parties. Enemy doing improvement to trenches	App
CHANTICLER	4/8/18		Wiring parties	App
CHANTICLER	5/8/18		Battalion relieved 5th Duke of Wellington's Regt in the left sub-section of the right section (see Operation Orders)	App 10
IN THE LINE	6/8/18		Operations in accordance with appendix 10	App 10
IN THE LINE	7/8/18		Operations in accordance with appendix 10	App
IN THE LINE	8/8/18		Battalion is relieved by L.R.B. proceeds to MAROEUIL (see appendix)	App 11
MAROEUIL	9/8/18		Battalion proceeds from MAROEUIL to MONCHY-BRETTON by rail en route ward. Arriv. MONCHY BRETTON 4.0 p.m. (See appendix 12)	App
MONCHY BRETON	10/8/18		Battalion in billets, cleaning up etc	App

Army Form C. 2118.

Original
WAR DIARY
or
INTELLIGENCE SUMMARY.

2/1st Duke of Wellington Regt

(Erase heading not required.)

Instructions regarding War Diaries and Intelligence Summaries are contained in F.S. Regs., Part II. and the Staff Manual respectively. Title pages will be prepared in manuscript.

Place	Date	Hour	Summary of Events and Information	Remarks and references to Appendices
MONCHY-BRETON.	11/9/18		Battalion leaves MONCHY-BRETON proceeds by route-march to TINCQUES. men & transport arrive & billets as lastscreen.	MM
TINCQUES.	12/9/18		Clearing-up, checking stores & Draft of 104 men arrive from England.	MM
TINCQUES.	13/9/18		Training Programme commenced. Lt. J. Dursley proceeded on leave to U.K.	MM
TINCQUES	14/9/18		Training as per programme. Specialist training under specialist officers. "A" Company firing on ranges. Captain W.C. Pigeon. Lieut. R. Tanner M.C. + Lt. Thornton proceeded on leave to U.K.	MM
TINCQUES	15/9/18		Training programme carried out. C.O's Parade. "B" Company firing on ranges. Band of 13th East Yorkshire Regiment reported to this Battalion for duty. The battalion is inoculated.	MM
TINCQUES.	16/9/18		Parades as usual, less inoculated men. Major England reports for duty this day.	MM

Army Form C. 2118.

Original
WAR DIARY
or
INTELLIGENCE SUMMARY.
(Erase heading not required.)

1/7th Duke of Wellington's Regt

Instructions regarding War Diaries and Intelligence Summaries are contained in F. S. Regs., Part II. and the Staff Manual respectively. Title pages will be prepared in manuscript.

Place	Date	Hour	Summary of Events and Information	Remarks and references to Appendices
TINQUES	17/9/18		Battalion on church parade. New band turns out for the first time.	Nil
TINQUES	18/9/18		Training programme carried out. "A" Company firing on range. "B" Company practising "Platoon in the Attack".	Nil
TINQUES	19/9/18		Battalion Parade. Training under specialist officers.	Nil
TINQUES	20/9/18		Training programme carried. Specialist training as usual.	Nil
TINQUES	21/9/18		"C" Company "Bullet & Bayonet" fighting course. "D" Company firing on the range. "A" Company practising Platoon scheme. Specialists of "B" & "C" Companies under their respective officers.	Nil
TINQUES	22/9/18		"D" Company on the range. "C" Company "Bullet & Bayonet" course. "A" Company practising Platoon scheme. Specialists of "B" & "C" Companies under their respective officers.	Nil
TINQUES	23/9/18		Training programme carried out. Specialist training. Battalion mounted for record King.	Nil

Army Form C. 2118.

Original
WAR DIARY
or
INTELLIGENCE SUMMARY.
(Erase heading not required.)

Instructions regarding War Diaries and Intelligence Summaries are contained in F. S. Regs., Part II. and the Staff Manual respectively. Title pages will be prepared in manuscript.

2/7th Duke of Wellingtons Regt

Place	Date	Hour	Summary of Events and Information	Remarks and references to Appendices
TINQUES	24/9/16		Battalion on Church Parade.	Nil
TINQUES	25/9/16		Two companies firing on the range. Two companies practicing company scheme.	Nil
TINQUES	26/9/16		Whole Battalion on scheme at training area. Very successful. Officer proceeds to U.K. on leave. Captain G.W.M. Miller proceeds to 1st Army Musketry School on a course.	Nil
TINQUES	27/9/16		Two companies firing on Range. 1 Company Bullet & Bayonet Course. 1 Company specialist training.	Nil
TINQUES	28/9/16		Battalion bathing. Training as on previous day. Night practice in forming up on tape line, and Company schemes from 6.30 to 9.30 p.m. Orders received for move to forward area.	Nil

Major
Commanding
2/7th Duke of Wellingtons Regt.

"War Diary"   Appendix 8.

OPERATION ORDERS
by
LIEUT-COLONEL W.B. STACKHAM, D.S.O., M.C., COMMANDING
/7th. BN. DUKE OF WELLINGTON'S REGIMENT.
IN THE FIELD.   THURSDAY,   31st. JANUARY 1918.
....

(1) Reference Operation Orders of 30.1.18.

(a) The Battalion will parade at 2.45 p.m. and proceed to the Support
     Area.
     Order of March will be :- 'B' Coy., 'A' Coy., 'C' Coy., 'D' Coy., H.Q.
     Dress will be :-
            'A' and 'B' Companies — Fighting Order. Packs will be worn.
            H.Q., 'C' and 'D' Companies — Marching Order.

(b) Para. 2 of Operation Orders of 30.1.18. is amended as follows:-
     'B' Company will relieve one Company of 2/5th. King's Own Yorkshire
     Light Infantry in BAILLEUL NORD and 'A' Company will relieve one
     Company of 2/5th. Bn. York & Lancs Regiment in THE LINE, North of
     GAVRELLE ROAD.

(c) Reference Para. 3 of Operation Orders of 30.1.18.
     For 'B' Company read 'D' Company.
     Guides for Lewis Gun Teams detailed in Para. 3 of yesterday's
     Operation Orders will be at the head of advanced train at
     BAILLEUL. at 2.0 p.m. to-morrow.
     These Teams will consist of 4 Other Ranks only.
     No guides will be provided for the remainder of the Battalion.

(d) O.C. 'A' Company will arrange to leave One N.C.O. and 3 Other Ranks

1.

of 'C' Company, 1 man from 'B' Company and 1 man from 'A' Company, who are manning the Brigade O.P. Orders for these men have been issued by the Intelligence Officer.

(3) Advance Parties will proceed so as to arrive at their respective positions by noon.

(Sgd) A. CAMPBELL, Captain & Adjutant,
2/7th. Bn. Duke of Wellington's Regiment.

War Diary   Appendix 9

OPERATION ORDERS
by
LIEUT.COLONEL W.S. MACFARLAN, D.S.O., T.D., COMMANDING
4/7th. BN. DUKE OF WELLINGTON'S REGIMENT.

IN THE FIELD.   SUNDAY.   3rd. FEBRUARY 1915.

(1) 'A' Company will move from its present billets to a position near Brigade Headquarters (B.I.C.) to-morrow, February 4th.
O.C. 'A' Company will arrange to arrive at the latter billets by 11.30 a.m.

(2) 1 Officer and 2 N.C.O's will be left behind to hand over stores, etc. to Unit of 147th. Infantry Brigade.

(3) Clearing Certificate and Frozen Store List will be forwarded to Battalion Headquarters by 3.0 p.m.

(4) Lieut. C. Tanner, R.O. and 2 N.C.O's from Battalion Headquarters will act as billeting party and report to Staff Captain at Brigade Headquarters at 9.30 a.m.
Lieut. C. Tanner, R.O. will arrange to meet 'A' Company on the outbound track at 11.15 a.m.

(5) The Mess Sergeant will arrange to have hot tea ready for this Company in Headquarters Camp at 12.30 p.m.

(6) Any stores which cannot be conveniently carried will be dumped at Company Ration Dump. O.C. 'A' Company will arrange with O.C. 'B' Company for a small party to load these stores on limbers to-morrow night under the supervision of one of the N.C.O's left behind to hand over. A list of such stores will be forwarded to Battalion Headquarters by 4 p.m. so that the necessary limbers may be detailed.

(7) Completion of relief will be reported to Battalion Headquarters as soon as possible.

(8) Orders for to-morrow night's working party will be issued later.

(Sgd) H. ORMROD, Captain & Adjutant,
4/7th. Bn. Duke of Wellington's Regiment.

Appendix 10.

OPERATION ORDERS
by
LIEUT.COLONEL F.S. THACKERAY, D.S.O., M.C., COMMANDING
2/7th. BN. DUKE OF WELLINGTON'S REGIMENT.

IN THE FIELD.   MONDAY.   4th. FEBRUARY 1918.
....

(1) The Battalion will relieve 5th. Duke of Wellington's Regiment in the left sub-section of the Right (GAVRELLE) Section on the night 5th/6th. February.

(2) Dispositions on completion of relief will be as follows :-
   MILL POST. }   Right Coy. 'D' Coy.
              }   Left Coy.   'B'
   BRADFORD POST. 'C' Coy, with Platoon 'A' Coy attached.
                   Support Coy - remainder of 'A' Coy in MARINE
                                                        TRENCH.
   Os.C.Companies will arrange minor dispositions.
   On completion of relief, Captain F.M.C. Shearme will be in command of MILL POST.

(3) 1 Platoon of 'A' Company will be attached to 'C' Company for tactical and administrative purposes.
   O.C. 'C' Company will be entirely responsible for this Platoon.
   O i/c this Platoon will report to O.C. 'C' Company at 2 p.m. to-morrow.
   Quartermaster will arrange re-distribution of rations.
   O.C. 'A' Company will notify Quartermaster number of men in this Platoon.

(4) An Advance Party of 1 Officer per Company, 1 N.C.O. per Platoon, Lieut. W.A. Hinchcliffe and 2 N.C.O's from Headquarters will be sent forward to arrive in new position by 10 a.m.

(5) Order of March will be :- 'C' Company, 1 Platoon 'A' Company, 'D' Company, 'B' Company, 'A' Company, Headquarters.
   Dress :- Fighting Order. Jerkins will be worn.
   'C' Company and 1 Platoon of 'A' Company will move off at 4.30 p.m. and meet guides at Cross-roads B.28.a.7.0. at 6.30 p.m.
   The remaining Companies and Headquarters will follow at usual distances to arrive at forward Battalion Headquarters to meet guides at 7 p.m.
   'B' Company will join the Battalion in its appointed place about B.28.c.6.4.

(6) Transport Officer will arrange to transport the 4 Lewis Guns of 'C' Company and 1 Lewis Gun of 'A' Company, which are going to BRADFORD POST, to CHANTICLER SIDING, by 3.30 p.m. These will proceed up the line with rations to-morrow night.
   A Lewis Gun Limber will report to O.C. 'D' Company to collect the guns in time for same to be taken up with rations to-morrow night.
   Transport Officer will notify Os.C.Companies arrangements with regard to rations and water.

(7) A runner from Headquarters will be detailed to report to O.C. 'A' Company to-morrow morning. O.C. 'A' Company will give him instructions, in writing, to proceed to each of his 3 Lewis Gun Posts, ordering them to proceed direct to Battalion Headquarters at B.30.a.0.5. by 7 p.m.
   1 man from each of these Teams will act as a guide to take back the relieving teams of 5th. Duke of Wellington's Regiment.

(8) Blankets, Packs, spare kits, etc. of 'A' Coy, 'C' Coy, 'D' Coy and Headquarters will be stacked by 2 p.m.
   Those of 'B' Coy will be stacked and left in charge of a Guard until limbers report at night.

(9) All Defence Schemes, Trench Maps, Trench Stores, etc. will be carefully taken over. Lists of above will be forwarded to Battalion Headquarters as soon as possible after relief.

(10) Completion of relief will be notified to Battalion Headquarters by EAR Coys.

(11) Gum Boots will be drawn from Battalion Headquarters for Sentries. Sentries will wear with Gum Boots 2 pairs of socks. Quartermaster will arrange for additional socks for this purpose.

(12) Working Parties provided by this Battalion will cease after the 7 a.m. parties.

(13) It is of the greatest importance that all Returns and Reports are rendered to Battalion Headquarters punctually.

(Sgd) R. ORMEROD, Captain & Adjutant,
2/7th. Bn. Duke of Wellington's Regiment.

Appendix "..."

OPERATION ORDERS

BY

LIEUT.-COLONEL R.E. TRACKERAY, ..., ..., COMMANDING
2/4TH. BN. DUKE OF WELLINGTON'S REGIMENT.

IN THE FIELD.   THURSDAY.   7th. FEBRUARY, 1918.

....

(1) The Battalion will be relieved in the line by the London Rifle Brigade on night 8th/9th. February.

(2) Companies will be relieved as under :-
'A' Coy, less 1 Platoon, 2/7th, by 'D' Coy, 18th & Platoon, L.R.B.
'B' Coy, 2/7th, by 'C' Coy, L.R.B.
'C' Coy and 1 Platoon 'A' Coy, 2/7th, by 'A' Coy & 1 Platoon, 'B' Coy, L.R.B.
'D' Coy, 2/7th. by 'B' Coy, L.R.B.

(3) Advance Parties of Incoming Unit will arrive about noon to take over quarters etc.
1 Runner from Headquarters and 1 man from each Company will meet Advance Parties at CHATEION at 10.30 a.m.

(4) The Battalion on relief will move to BANDBULL by Trench Tram as follows:-
'A' Coy, less 1 Platoon, will entrain at CHESTERFIELD at 8 p.m.
H.Q. Coy. will entrain at CHATERION at 9 p.m.
'B' Coy will entrain at CHATERION at 10.00 p.m.
'D' Coy will entrain at CHATERION at 10.30 p.m.
'C' Coy and 1 Platoon 'A' Coy. will entrain at Harley Lodge,
B.M.G.O.S. at 11.30 p.m.

(5) 'A', 'B' and 'D' Companies will send Platoon Guides to Battalion Headquarters at 2 p.m., they will march across under Sgt. Holloway, to meet incoming Unit at the end of the SKIDECK Track at P.A.C.B.
Guides will be furnished as under :-
'B' and 'D' Companies, 4 Guides.
'A' Company, 3 Guides.
'C' Company will send 4 Platoon Guides to meet incoming Unit at Harley, hutting camp B.M.G.T.
One Guide from 'C' Company will show the Lewis position in NORTH TYNE ALLEY as the incoming Unit has 2 Platoons per Company.

(6) All Trench Stores, Ammunition, Supplies and Water in Supporting Points will be handed over and receipts obtained not by incoming and outgoing Companies and handed over to A.E.S.Q.M.S. (in duplicate) duly completed will be forwarded to Battalion Headquarters as soon as possible.
1 copy of A.E.Q.M.Q. returns in duplicate to Companies, the remaining copies being completed on plain paper.
White Overall Suits for Patrols will be sent to Quartermaster to-night, who will hand same to A.E.Q.M.S. first opportunity after relief and obtain receipt.
Water and Petrol Cans, Lamp boxes Carried and other carts, and all Dyer's stoves will be handed over to relieving Unit by Quartermaster.

(7) All Defence Schemes will be handed over to relieving Unit.
All extract Trench Maps used above 1/10,000 and 1/40,000 Enemy's line area will be handed over to relieving Unit, 1/40,000 maps will be retained.
Work in hand and proposed work will be carefully handed over.
Lists of Maps handed over will be forwarded to Battalion Headquarters as soon as possible.

1.

(7) Stores and Lewis Guns.
    RATIONS. The train bringing up rations for incoming Unit
    will take down Lewis Guns and spare stores of this Unit.
    Transport Officer will arrange to collect these at [illegible]
    [illegible] and convey to HARDECUL.
    AMMUNITION. All Lewis Guns and surplus stores will be handed
    as soon as possible after relief to Ration Dump. Transport
    Officer will arrange to collect same at this point and convey to
    HARDECUL. Lewis guns will be taken to Wagon Lines.

(8) All Petrol Tins and Gun Boots will be at Ration Dump by 5 p.m.
    and a receipt obtained from the R.Q.M.S.
    Quartermaster will arrange to hand in to Divisional Gas Mask Store,
    BORDIGHONT, all Gas Boots & other items and obtain receipts.

(9) An Advance Party of Lieut. W. Tatham, M.O., 1 N.C.O. from Headquarters
    and 1 N.C.O. per Company will leave Battalion Headquarters at 6 a.m.
    to catch the train leaving QUARTIER at 10 a.m. These N.C.O's
    should be in possession of State Rooms (a) No. of Officers (b) No.
    of O.Rs. to be billeted.

(10) 2/Lieut. G. Mattersley, 1 N.C.O. per Company and 1 N.C.O. from
     Headquarters, Transport Section and Quartermaster Stores will
     entrain at HARDECUL at 4.15 p.m. This party (except N.C.O's from
     Transport Section and Quartermaster's Stores, who will report to
     2/Lieut. G. Mattersley at HARDECUL) will leave Battalion Headquarters
     with 2/Lieut. G. Mattersley at 2 p.m.
     This party will proceed to take over billets to be occupied by this
     Unit at FOREST L'EVEQUE on February 8th and report to Area Commandant,
     HARDECUL.

(11) Transport Officer will arrange to have [illegible] leave, Lewis
     packs and blankets conveyed to new area.
     2 G.S. Wagons will report at him at 1.30 p.m. for this purpose.

(12) Quartermaster will arrange to have hot tea for Companies and
     Headquarters on arrival.

(13) Completion of relief will be reported to these Headquarters in due
     code.

(14) Battalion and Transport will move on February 9th. to the FOREST
     L'EVEQUE area.

(15) Baggage Wagons of Reg. Lime Transport will report on 9th. inst.
     and will move with Regimental Transport.

(16) 5 Motor Lorries have been applied for. Details will be issued by
     Quartermaster.

(17) All area and billet stores will be handed over to incoming Unit,
     Receipts obtained and countersigned by the Area Commandant or Town
     Major.
     Detailed receipts showing correction location of all Water
     and Iron Rations held in the Defence Scheme, Parts or Support line
     will be obtained from relieving Unit and forwarded to Battalion
     Headquarters in duplicate.

(18) Clearing Certificate for Store issued will be obtained from Area
     Commandant or relieving Unit.

(19) Arrival in new billets will be reported to Battalion Headquarters
     as soon as possible.

(20) ACKNOWLEDGE.

                                    (Sgd) R. OLDFIELD, Captain & Adjutant,
                                    2/7th. Bn. Duke of Wellington's Regiment).

OPERATION ORDERS
by
LIEUT-COLONEL E.S. THACKERAY, D.S.O., M.C., COMMANDING
2/4th. Bn. DUKE OF WELLINGTON'S REGIMENT.
IN THE FIELD.   SATURDAY.   9th. FEBRUARY 1918.
....

(1) The Battalion will move from MAROEUIL to TINQUES by rail and thence
    to MONCHY BRETON Area by route march to-day, February 9th.

(2) Companies will march independently to MAROEUIL Station and report
    there in the following order and times:-
        Headquarters.   12.20 p.m.
        'A' Coy.   12.22 p.m.
        'B' Coy.   12.24 p.m.
        'C' Coy.   12.26 p.m.
        'D' Coy.   12.28 p.m.
    Dress:- Full Marching Order. Steel Helmets will be worn.

(3) Companies will render Marching Out State to Battalion Orderly Room
    by 10.30 a.m. showing number of Other Ranks to be entrained.
    A consolidated State will be made and handed to 2/Lieut. Scott, who
    will report to R.T.O. 10 minutes before Battalion arrives at the
    Station.
    A N.C.O. per truck will be detailed by O's.C.Companies and H.Q., to
    prevent men from leaving the train without permission.

(4) Transport will move under orders of Transport Officer.

(5) Particular attention will be paid to maintaining strict march
    discipline.
    200 yards distance will be kept between Companies.

(6) Quartermaster will detail guides to meet Motor Lorries at Brigade
    Wagon Lines at 8.30 a.m.

(7) Blankets, spare stores, etc. will be dumped at some convenient place
    near each Company Headquarters and Battalion Headquarters by 8.30 a.m.
    and a runner sent to Battalion Headquarters to guide Lorry to these
    Dumps.

(8) Arrival in billets will be notified to Orderly Room as early as
    possible.

                                    (Sgd) A. ORMEROD, Captain & Adjutant,
                                          2/4th Bn. Duke of Wellington's Regiment.

62nd Division.
186th Infantry Brigade

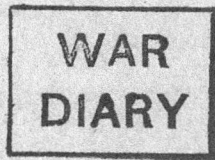

2/7th BATTALION

DUKE OF WELLINGTON'S REGIMENT

MARCH 1 9 1 8

SECRET

Vol 15

156/62

Lt Vert

15+
12 details

2/4th Bn. Duke of Wellingtons (W.R) Regt

Original

WAR DIARY.

From :- 1st March 1918
To :- 31st March 1918

rendered in accordance with F.S. Regs Part II.

VOLUME XV.

E. S. Shuker
Lieut Colonel
Comg
2/4th Duke of Wellingtons Regiment

1.4.1918.

Original

Army Form C. 2118.

WAR DIARY
or
INTELLIGENCE SUMMARY.   2/4th Duke of Wellington's Regt.
(Erase heading not required.)

Place	Date	Hour	Summary of Events and Information	Remarks and references to Appendices
TINCQUES.	1/3/18		Orders received for move towards the forward area. Lieut. Burton and billeting party proceeded to BRAY CAMP at ECOIVRES to take over camp of 3rd Coldstream Guards. Battalion took part in a Brigade Tactical Scheme north of CHELERS. Returned to billets about 1.0 p.m. and arrangements made for move on the day following.	(W)
do	2/3/18		Battalion proceeded to ECOIVRES by train leaving TINCQUES at 11.0 am. Arrived 12.30 p.m. Transport proceeded by road and arrived at noon. Arrangements in accordance with Appendix 1. Good camp. Weather very cold.	(W)
ECOIVRES.	3/3/18		Snow, very cold. Reveille 5am. Battalion entrained at Lower Siding at 9.30 am and detrained at THELUS. Thence by march to the line to relieve the 10th East Yorkshire Regiment in the ACHEVILLE SECTION. "C" Coy in Support, "D" Coy in Reserve. Trenches in first rate condition. Transport located at ECURIE. Arrangements for relief in accordance with Appendix 2.	Appen 1 Ref Map 36.C Squares 72.4. 73.0 (W) Appen II
Line	4/3/18		In the line. C.& D. Coy furnished working parties & patrols. A patrol of 1 Officer & 12 O.R. went out from H.q. Ref. 72.4. G. 75.50. & proceeded East to Sunken road. Thence Northwards, parallel to our line for 600 yds. Thence Westwards to WINNIPEG RD. Returned to Battalion Headquarters. No enemy were encountered. No country down the road. Patrol leader:- 2/Lt N.T. Marsh. Pass Word. WHISKEY.	Squares 72.4. 73.0 (W)

WAR DIARY
or
INTELLIGENCE SUMMARY

Army Form C. 2118.

Place	Date	Hour	Summary of Events and Information	Remarks and references to Appendices
LINE	4.3.18		A patrol of 1 Officer + 12 O.Rks. left our line at No 2 Post T30.6.0.6.9.3. proceeded EAST for 60 yds. thence due NORTH for 350 yds. Return by sunken road between 6 + 7 posts. Object to engage any hostile patrol to investigate 6.C. Patrol Leader Lt. A. MALLALIEU. No enemy were encountered. No casualties. C + D Coy provided working parties + patrols. Naval Trench Centre.	Left map B6.C. SOCKS
LINE	5.3.18		At 13 worked on front line road and patrols. Patrol left No 6 Post + proceeded via sunken road 200 yds. NORTH of this road for engagement of hostile Patrol came in contact 200 yds. NORTH for 100 yds. NORTH of sunken road to cover ground for examined same for 100 yds. NORTH of sunken road. No enemy patrols were encountered. No casualties. At Day provided patrol 1 Officer + 12 ORks. A patrol of 1 NCO + 8 men. Standing patrol + proceeded 300 yds due SOUTH + lay in wait for any small enemy patrol was encountered by mine to No 1 post. Patrol reported noises of a body of enemy times, patrol returned to 1 Post. No casualties. D Coy provided patrol A patrol of 1 NCO + 6 men left No 16 Post T24.a.50.6.8. Standing patrol to proceed 300 yds. N.N.EAST + lie in wait for any small patrol concealed by mine to hold Post. Patrol returned. No casualties. No enemy encountered. Patrol was provided by 13 Coy.	

Original

WAR DIARY 2/7 Duke of Wellington Rgt
or
INTELLIGENCE SUMMARY.

Army Form C. 2118.

(Erase heading not required.)

Instructions regarding War Diaries and Intelligence Summaries are contained in F. S. Regs., Part II. and the Staff Manual respectively. Title pages will be prepared in manuscript.

Place	Date	Hour	Summary of Events and Information	Remarks and references to Appendices
LINE	5.3.18		A patrol left Battalion Headquarters & proceeded up WINNIPEG ROAD to the right post of Battalion on our left. Patrol returned without casualties. Patrol left before midnight. 2nd Patrol left after midnight & returned 5.30 same route. Patrols consisted of 1 officer 12 O.R.s. provided by C Coy.	Left the p.36.C. T24.T30
LINE	6.3.18		Usual trench routine. Distanding patrol went out from No.1 post. T30.a.98.74 & proceeded 300 yds due SOUTH & lay in wait for any small enemy patrol. No enemy were encountered. Patrol returned by the 1 Post Large of Patrol 1 NCO & 6 O.R.s. A patrol of 1 NCO & 6 men left No.16 post at T24.a.50.68 & proceeded 300 yds NNEAST & lay in wait for any small enemy patrols. No enemy patrol were encountered, patrol returned by No.16 post. Other patrols as ordered the night previous.	NIL
LINE	7.3.18		Usual trench Routine. Weather fine, slight haze, observation difficult. Work carried out on first line trenches by A + B Coys. C.Ts & Support trenches by C + D Coys. Patrols were sent out as on the previous nights. The Left Lewis Gun Patrol was withdrawn, & a Stationary patrol 1 NCO & 6 men sent out. A patrol 1 Officer & 12 O.R.s. were sent from this Battalion on our Right Flank. Found quiet, left soon after midnight returned unmolested. Casualties Nil.	E.I.

Original

WAR DIARY 2nd/7th Bn Duke of Wellington Regt
or
INTELLIGENCE SUMMARY.

Army Form C. 2118.

Place	Date	Hour	Summary of Events and Information	Remarks and references to Appendices
LINE	8.3.18		Meant head Routine Patrol of 1 Officer + 12 O.R's went out from No 2 Post at T30.b.06.93 + proceeded EAST 60 yds, then due NORTH 300 yds. Patrol returned by sunken road between No's 6 + 7 Post. No enemy were encountered. Casualties nil. Patrol leader 2Lt A B Smith	MH
	9.3.18		The Battalion was relieved by the 2/4 Duke of Wellington Regt. The relief was completed by 2-5PM. Battalion moved to SPRINGVALE Camp in Brigade Reserve. Route. Hudson C.T. C.P.R. TRENCH. MERSEY C.T. duckboard track to ARRAS. LENS ROAD to SPRINGVALE CAMP. The Battalion arrived at the camp at 4.30PM	MH
SPRINGVALE CAMP	10.3.18		Weather fine. Inspection parades.	MH
	11.3.18		Ordinary Regimental Routine	MH
-	12.3.18		Ordinary Regimental Routine	MH
-	13.3.18		Ordinary Regimental Routine	MH
-	14.3.18		Weather fine. Inspection Parades etc.	MH
-	15.3.18		The Battalion moved into the line relieved 5th Bn Duke of Wellington Regt. See appendix copy No J.3.	copy to G. Ahrens 3
LINE	16.3.18			
	17.3.18		A highly successful raid was carried out by 80 men of "B" Company under the command of Lt. N. L. HOPPER + 2Lt. J. BUCKLEY in which 5 enemy	Map with 51B.N.W. MH
	18.3.18			

Army Form C. 2118.

WAR DIARY
or
INTELLIGENCE SUMMARY.
(Erase heading not required.)

Head Quarters Duke of Wellington's Bn

Instructions regarding War Diaries and Intelligence Summaries are contained in F.S. Regs., Part II. and the Staff Manual respectively. Title pages will be prepared in manuscript.

Place	Date	Hour	Summary of Events and Information	Remarks and references to Appendices
LINE	18/3/18		Prisoners were captured. We had two casualties 1 killed & 1 wounded. Full particulars will be found in Appendix Copy No. 3.A.	Copy left by Lt [?] Appendix No 3A
LINE.	19/3/18		Ordinary routine while in support. Lieut. W.A. HINCHCLIFFE arrived from sniping course. Lieut LOWTHER arrived from general course.	No 3A
"	20/3/18		In support. Ordinary routine.	No 3A
"	21/3/18		Battalion moved up into the front line relieved 6th Bn. DUKE OF WELLINGTON'S REGT. We were relieved by 2/4th Bn Duke of Wellington Regt.	No 3A Wellington's
"	22/3/18		Ordinary trench routine. Very quiet. Weather good. At night 5 of 91/3nd & 22nd/23rd. 5 Patrols went out as follows: 1st Patrol. 1 officer + 16 other ranks went out from T 34 a 93.68. Reconnoitred our wire. Established liaison with 52nd Canadian Bn at T 17 d. 65.75. They left at 10.30 p.m. returned at 2 a.m. to the same place. Nothing extraordinary happened. 2nd Patrol of 1 N.C.O. & men + 1 L.G. left T 34 a 93.68 established a listening post about 200 yards north of T 34 a 93.68 where they could observe between HUDSON POST. The Canadians, to 3 Patrol of 1 Officer + 5 O.R. left T 34 a 35.86 + established a listening post of 1 officer + 5 O.R. left T 34 a 00.40. The ordinary trench routine was heard they went out at 1.30 a.m. returned at 5 a.m. to the starting point. No 4 Patrol of 1 officer + 5 O.R. left T 34 d 03.13. Proceeded to about T 30 c 45.95. They left Act 12.30 a.m. returned to the starting point at 4.30 a.m. Everything was absolutely quiet no unusual movement was heard. They left map S1 B N W. No 3A	map S1 B N W No 3A

WAR DIARY
or
INTELLIGENCE SUMMARY.
(Erase heading not required.)

Army Form C. 2118.

Place	Date	Hour	Summary of Events and Information	Remarks and references to Appendices
LINE	22/3/18		No. 5 Patrol of 1 officer + 16 O.R. left 30 B.00.92 at 10.30 a.m. to establish liaison with 7th West Yorkshire Regiment on our right. Line wire was also connected + found to be in a bad state. They returned to the starting point at 4.30 a.m. having accomplished their mission.	map S/13 N.W.
	23/3/18		The battalion was relieved in the line by the 58th Canadian Battalion + proceeded to BOIS-des-ALLEUX, MONT ST. ELOI by HUDSON CT. C.P.R.C.T. + MERSEY ALLEY then by light railway from THELUS. The battalion was all in Camp Hutted down by 10.0 P.M.	A.H.
MONT ST ELOI	04/5/18		The battalion marched to "Y" Huttments near DUISANS were in camp at 4.30 P.M. except "B" Company who arrived at 2.0 a.m.	A.H.
DUISANS	25/3/18		The battalion left DUISANS at 10 a.m. marched to BUCQUOY where they took up a defensive position behind ACHIET-LE-PETIT in front of BUCQUOY.	A.H.
LINE	26/3/18		The enemy made three distinct attacks on BUCQUOY, all of which were driven off by our rifle, machine gun fire. Many enemy parties were seen wavering on the PUISIEUX - ACHIET-LE-PETIT road.	A.H.
"	27/3/18		Battalion still in the same position. Much enemy transport seen own S.S.W from ACHIET-LE-PETIT	A.H.

Original

Army Form C. 2118.

WAR DIARY
or
INTELLIGENCE SUMMARY.

(Erase heading not required.)

Instructions regarding War Diaries and Intelligence Summaries are contained in F. S. Regs., Part II. and the Staff Manual respectively. Title pages will be prepared in manuscript.

2/7 Duke of Wellington Rgt

Place	Date	Hour	Summary of Events and Information	Remarks and references to Appendices
LINE	26/3/18		The battalion on our right is the 2/4th D.L.W.Regt. The battalion on our left is the 2/7th West Yorkshire Regiment	A.H
-	27/3/18		Enemy shelled us very heavily. Counter attack by enemy on our right successfully broken off, causing him many casualties.	A.H
-	28/3/18		More enemy shelling. More attacks which were successfully beaten off	A.H
-	29/3/18		Situation much the same.	A.H
-	30/3/18		Usual shelling. Enemy attacks, which were all beaten off.	A.H
-	31/3/18		The battalion is relieved in the line by a battalion of the 87th Division came out to SOYAST NE. During their tour in the line, the battalion successfully beat off several enemy attacks, captured about 30 prisoners and four machine guns, two light machine & complete	

WAR DIARY
or
INTELLIGENCE SUMMARY.

Army Form C. 2118.

Place	Date	Hour	Summary of Events and Information	Remarks and references to Appendices
LINE.	31/3/16		Two heavy warnings LIEUT. H.L. HOPPER + LIEUT J BUCKLEY awarded the military cross. During this period very heavy casualties were inflicted on the enemy by our rifle & Lewis gun fire. H.S. Thacker Lieut Colonel Cmdt 2/4th Duke of Wellington's Regiment	N4.

War Diary, Appendix I

War Diary Appendix I/2.3.18

SECRET.   Copy No. 9

2/7th Bn. DUKE OF WELLINGTON'S
(W.R.) REGIMENT (OPERATION) ORDER No. 3.
....

1. The Battalion will relieve the 10th East Yorkshire Regiment in Section L.2. to-morrow the 3rd instant.

2. On completion of relief, Companies will be disposed as under:-
   "A" Coy.   Right Front ("A" Coy. 10th E.Y.R.)
   "B" Coy.   Left Front, ("C" Coy.   )
   "C" Coy.   Support in BRANDON TRENCH ("B" Coy. 10th E.Y.R.)
   "D" Coy.   Reserve in KIT BRUNSWICK ("D" Coy.   ).

3. The Battalion will parade at 6.45 a.m.
   Dress:- Fighting Order. Jerkins will be worn, greatcoats carried bandolier.

4. The Battalion will entrain at Tower Siding at 7.30 a.m. and detrain at TRALUC.

5. One guide will meet the Battalion at this point. Platoon guides will report to Platoons at the junction of HUDSON TRENCH and VANCOUVER ROAD.

6. Order of march from detraining point will be:-
   "B" Company.
   "A"   "
   Headquarters.
   "C" Company.
   "D"   "

   Fifty yards will be maintained between Platoons.

7. Route:- Detraining Point - MERSEY - C.P.H.TRENCH - HUDSON TRENCH.

8. All defence Schemes, Aeroplane Photographs, Maps, details of work and proposals for work will be taken over.

9. All Trench Stores will be taken over and a complete list of these Stores will be forwarded to Battalion Headquarters by 8.0 p.m. on March 3rd.

10. During progress of relief, Lewis Guns, Stretchers etc. will not be carried on the shoulder. No movement must take place over the open East of the West entrance to JERSEY ALLEY.

11. Companies will take over Cook Mess and Position Calls of the Companies they relieve.

12. Completion of relief will be reported in B.A.B.Code.

13. Unconsumed portion of the day's rations will be carried on the man. Water bottles will be filled before leaving present billets.

14. All blankets, Officers' kitbags, men's packs etc. will be stacked at the Quartermaster's Stores by 6.00 a.m.

15. Transport will take over Transport Lines of the 10th East Yorkshire Regiment.

                                    /Sgd/ H. ORMROD, Captain & Adjutant.
                                    2/7th Bn. Duke of Wellington's Regiment.

Copy No. 1. C.O.   Copy No. 2. O.C. "A" Coy.
  "   " 3. O.C. "B" Coy.   "   " 4. O.C. "C" Coy.
  "   " 5. O.C. "D" Coy.   "   " 6. T.O. and Q.M.
  "   " 7. M.S.M.   "   " 8. Details.
  "   " 9. War Diary.   "   " 10. File.

Appendix 3

Copy No... 9...

2/7th. Bn. DUKE OF WELLINGTON'S REGIMENT.

(OPERATION) ORDER NO. 7.

1. The Battalion, less 'B' Company, will move into Support to-morrow and relieve the 5th. Duke of Wellington's Regiment.

2. Companies will relieve as under :-
   'A' Coy. relieve 'D' Coy of 5th. D. of W's Regt.
   'C' "   "   'B' "   ditto.
   'D' "   "   'A' "   ditto.
   'B' Company will remain in SPRINGVALE CAMP.

3. On completion of relief, Companies will be disposed as under :-
   'A' Company - CANADA NORTH.
   'C'   "   - CANADA SOUTH.
   'D'   "   - STRONG POINTS known as SHEFFIELD, WAKEFIELD,
                 BARNSLEY and BEEHIVE.
                 Company Headquarters at BEEHIVE.

4. Guides - as arranged by O.C. Companies.

5. One Company of the 2/4th. Bn. D. of W's Regt. will relieve one Coy of 5th. D. of W's Regt. and will have one Platoon in COVENT S.P. and three Platoons in RAILWAY EMBANKMENT.

6. O.C. 'C' Coy will arrange to relieve COVENT S.P. by 5.0 a.m. to-morrow (15th.) with one Platoon. This Platoon after being relieved at dusk by a Platoon of the 2/4th. D. of W's Regt., will rejoin their Company in CANADA SOUTH.

7. O.C. 'D' Company will arrange to relieve SHEFFIELD S.P. by 5.0 a.m. to-morrow.

8. The reliefs of 'C' and 'D' Companies will be completed by 10.30 a.m.

9. 'A' Company and Battalion Headquarters will parade at SPRINGVALE CAMP at 8.10 a.m. and move to the Support Area via ARRAS - LONG ROAD - DUCKBOARD TRACK - MUSHY C.T. - C.P.S. TRENCH - HUDSON TRENCH.

10. Dress for all the Battalion :- Fighting Order with Greatcoats rolled round the haversack.

11. Intelligence Officer, Signalling Officer and Adjutant will report to O.C. 5th. Bn. D. of W's Regiment by 10.0 a.m.

12. All (1) Defence Schemes, (2) Aeroplane Photographs, (3) Maps, (4) Details of work (5) Proposals for work, will be carefully taken over.

13. All Trench Stores will be carefully handed over and taken over and a complete list of these stores forwarded to Bn. H.Q. as early as possible. O.C. 'C' Company will hand over the ammunition sent up to-night on a separate list.

14. Q.M. will take over all ration arrangements from 5th. Bn. of ? Regt.

15. Completion of relief will be reported by the word "GUMBOATS".

16. During progress of relief, Lewis Guns, Stretchers, etc. will not be carried on the shoulder. All movement will be by communication Trench East of entrance to ?

17. Blankets, Valises, Packs and all surplus stores etc. will be stacked in Company Dumps by 4.0 a.m. The Transport Officer will arrange to collect.

18. 2/Lieut. G.H. Barraclough will remain in Camp to hand over to the incoming Unit. Coy. Commanders and the R.S.M. will forward a Certificate to Orderly Room by 7.45 a.m. that all Billets are left in a clean and sanitary condition. 2/Lt. Barraclough will obtain a Certificate to that effect from the incoming Unit or from the Area Commandant.

          (Sgd) H.ORMEROD, Captain & Adjutant,
               5/7th. Bn. Duke of Wellington's Regiment.

14.4.18.

Copies to :-

No. 1. Commanding Officer.   No. 2. O.C. 'A' Coy.
No. 3. O.C. 'B' Coy.   No. 4. O.C. 'C' Coy.
No. 5. O.C. 'D' Coy.   No. 6. T.O. and Q.M.
No. 7. R.S.M.   No. 8. 5th. Bn. of ? Regt.
No. 9. War Diary.   No.10. Details and File.

SECRET. *War Diary*

appendix H

To Recipients of 2/7th Bn Duke of Wellington's

Operation Order No 8.

ZERO will be at 11 p.m.

Please acknowledge.

H Ormerod

Capt & Adjt
2/7th Bn Duke of Wellington's Regt

17.3.1918.

War Diary   Copy No....14.

2/7th Bn. DUKE OF WELLINGTON'S REGIMENT.

(OPERATION) ORDER No. 8.

Reference Log Map 1a. - FRESNOY PARK.

1. The Battalion will carry out a raid on the enemy front line Trench on the night 17/18th March 1918.

2. OBJECTIVES:- Enemy front line T.24.d.52.00 to T.24.d.42.35.
                     Support Trench T.24.d.64.00 to T.24.d.63.15.
                     TULIP C.T. from T.24.d.63.15 to T.24.d.34.24.

3. OBJECT:- (1) To obtain prisoners and identification.
                (2) To inflict casualties.

4. Composition of raiding party:-
     Personnel will be found from "B" Company.
     Officer i/c:- Lieut. H. L. HOPPER and two orderlies.
Party (a). To clean up front line trench:- 4 N.C.Os and 24 men (divided into two parties of 2 N.C.Os and 12 men).
Party (b). To clean up Support Trench and Tulip Trench:- 2/Lieut. J. Buckley, 2 N.C.Os and 12 men.
Party (c). To form block at T.24.d.52.00:- 1 N.C.O. and 6 men.
Party (d). To form block at T.24.d.42.35:- 1 N.C.O. and 6 men.
Party (e). To capture gap at T.30.b.47.95:- 1 N.C.O. and 6 men.
Party (f). To escort prisoners:- 1 N.C.O. and 2 men.
To search trench for identifications:- 4 O.Rks.
Stretcher bearers:- 4 O.Rks.

Each of the parties (a), (c) and (d) will be accompanied by 2 O.Rks to lay tapes and to guide parties returning through the wire, and two sappers carrying a bangalore torpedo to complete gap if necessary.
     Total party:- 2 Officers, 10 N.C.Os, 66 men, 6 sappers.

5. Dress:- Officers:- Revolver, whistle, electric torch and luminous watch.
Other Ranks:- Rifle, fixed bayonets, 10 rounds S.A.A. in the rifle, 10 rounds in the breast pocket, two No. 5 Mills grenades in side pockets (except N.C.Os) wire breakers.
N.C.Os will carry one P. Bomb and electric torch.
Blocking parties (c) and (d) will each carry 24 No. 5 Mills grenades and 12 No. 23 grenades.
Parties (b) and (e) will carry 12 No. 5 Mills grenades and 6 No. 23 grenades.

Men of Party (f) to collect identifications will carry haversacks.
N.C.Os to carry large long-handled wire cutters.
Cap comforters will be worn by all parties.
Bayonets will be blacked.

6. **Wire-cutting.**
   (a) Gaps will be cut in enemy wire at T.24.d.45.00, T.24.d.40.12 and in front of Support Trenches at T.24.d.57.10. A gap at T.24.d.35.35. will be cut by means of the bangalore torpedo.
   (b) Two or more gaps will be cut in enemy wire in C.7.a.
   (c) Wire cutting will be extended over four days.
   Our wire. Three gaps will be cut in our wire approximately opposite Nos 3, 4 and 5 Posts and guide wires laid out through these gaps. Lieut. E.Tanner M.C. will be in charge of this duty.
   Strength of party for this service:- 3 N.C.Os and 9 men.
   O. C. 5th Bn. D. of W's Regt will cut gaps in our wire in rear of No. 1 Post and in front of SOUTH TRIUMPH and will lay tape through gaps from No. 1 Post to HART STREET for raiding party to return by.

7. **Method of attack.**
   (a) Gaps will be cut in our wire by Zero minus 1 hour as detailed above.
   (b) At zero minus 1 hour the raiding party will assemble in our front line trench.
   (c) At zero minus ten minutes the raiding party will commence to leave the trench and the head of each party will halt immediately West of the gaps in our wire. The formation to be adopted is shown in attached table.
   (d) At zero, barrage will come down on enemy front line - raiding party will close up to barrage.
   (e) At zero plus five minutes, barrage will lift off front line - raiding party will pass as rapidly as possible through enemy wire and enter trench.
   (f) At zero plus 20 minutes, party withdraws from enemy trench.
   (g) At zero plus 30 minutes, barrage slackens to slow rate of fire.
   (h) At zero plus 40 minutes barrage stops.

8. **Detail for individual parties.**
   "A" party to divide outwards and clean up front line trench as far as blocks.
   "B" Party will cross over front line trench and enter Support Trench and will establish a block at it's junction with TULIP TRENCH. As soon as the Support Trench is cleared, this party will work outwards down TULIP TRENCH as far as it's junction with front line where they will remain as a block till party "A" has completed it's task.
   Note:- Parties "A" and "B" not to use bombs except in emergency.
   "C" and "D" Parties to form blocks as detailed.

"E" Party. After capturing advanced Post at T.30.b.47.95, to protect right flank.

"F" Party. Prisoners will be escorted back as soon as captured.

9. At zero plus 20 minutes the Regimental Call will be sounded on bugles in our front line.
O. C. Raid will immediately shout out "YORKSHIRE" which will be passed on from man to man.
The whole party will then withdraw through same gaps by which they entered.
Tape will be laid from gaps in enemy wire to enemy front line trench.
After reaching our line all ranks will return via No. 1 Post to HART TRENCH.
O. C. 5th Bn. D. of W's Regt. will give instructions for this route to be taped and will detail four men as guides from No. 1 Postback.

10. RENDEZVOUS. All ranks will assemble at M.T.M. Headquarters dugout at T.28.b.90.75.
Route from front line will be HART TRENCH - BRANDON TRENCH - MONTREAL TRENCH.
O. C. 5th Bn. D. of W's Regt will detail the following to direct men back:-
   2 men at junction of BRANDON and HUDSON.
   2 men at junction of HUDSON and MONTREAL.
   2 men at junction of MONTREAL and BULFORD.

11. Protection of flanks. O. C. 5th Bn. D. of W's Regt will place Lewis Guns at about T.30.b.05.85 and T.24.d.15.45. to sweep NO MAN'S LAND on either flank of raiding party.

12. Barrage. Barrage programme attached - Appendix "A".

13. Great care must be taken that no wounded men are left behind in enemy trench. All ranks must assist in clearing casualties after retire signal has gone. Walking wounded will be treated at the small dugout at approximately T.24.d.0.5.
Stretcher cases:- Detail will be issued later.

14. SYNCHRONIZING OF WATCHES. All watches, including those of Artillery, M.T.Ms, L.T.Ms and M.Gs will be synchronized at 12 noon and 6.0 p.m. on the 17th inst at Brigade Headquarters.

15. The raiding party will assemble in Battalion Headquarters dugout in WINNIPEG ROAD at 8.30 p.m.

16. Preliminary arrangements.
(a) All ranks will make a daylight reconnaisance.

(b) All identifications to be removed from those taking part in the raid.
(c) Telephone communication.
(d) O. C. 5th Bn. D. of W's Regt will arrange for four stretchers to be placed in No. 4 Post prior to zero.
(e) O. C. 5th Bn. D. of W's Regt will arrange for concertina wire to be placed in rear of front line trench to fill up gaps in our wire cut for use of raiding party.
(f) Motor lorry to convey party from Springvale Camp to Duckboard Track and back again.

/Sgd/ NORMAN A. ENGLAND. Major.
Commanding,
2/7th Bn. Duke of Wellington's Regiment.

15.3.1918.

Copy No.		
" "	1.	Commanding Officer.
" "	2.	Lieut. H. L. Hopper.
" "	3.	2/Lieut. J. Buckley.
" "	4.	62nd Division.
" "	5.	186th Infantry Brigade.
" "	6.	5th Bn. D. of W's Regt.
" "	7.	C. R. A.
" "	8.	C. R. E.
" "	9.	D.T.M.O.
" "	10.	A.D.M.S.
" "	11.	186th L.T.M.B.
" "	12.	185th Infantry Brigade.
" "	13.	Machine Gun Battalion.
" "	14.	War Diary.
" "	15.	File.

62nd Division.
186th Infantry Brigade.

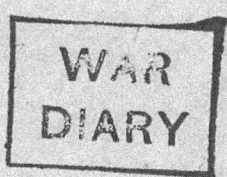

2/7th BATTALION

THE DUKE OF WELLINGTON'S REGIMENT

APRIL 1918

Appendices attached:-
    Operation Orders.
    Rewards.

Original

Army Form C. 2118.

Instructions regarding War Diaries and Intelligence Summaries are contained in F.S. Regs., Part II. and the Staff Manual respectively. Title pages will be prepared in manuscript.

WAR DIARY
or
INTELLIGENCE SUMMARY.
(Erase heading not required.)

2/7th Duke of Wellington's Regt.

Place	Date	Hour	Summary of Events and Information	Remarks and references to Appendices
SOUASTRE	1/11/18		Battalion in billets, cleaning up etc.	MR.
	2/11/18		Battalion left SOUASTRE at 1.30 p.m. + arrived in PAS-EN-ARTOIS at about 3.0 p.m.	MR.
PAS.	3/11/18		Cleaning up, inspections etc.	MR.
	4/11/18		Inspections, cleaning up etc. Companies at disposal of O's C Companies.	MR.
	5/11/18		Working party of 350 strong trench-digging on the SOUASTRE-FONQUEVILLERS road. Battalion strength - 15.	MR.
	6/11/18		Companies at disposal of O's C Companies.	MR.
	7/11/18		Battalion moved up the line relieved 1/11 Manchester Regiment in front of ABLAINZEVILLE.	MR.
line	8/11/18		Weather wet, visibility bad, much mud.	MR.
	9/11/18		In trenches, condition of same very bad.	MR.
	10/11/18		Weather better. 1/5 Lancashire Fusiliers battalion on right, 1/5 D of W. Regt battalion on right.	MR.
	11/11/18		Much trouble by hostile artillery sniping, movement impossible by day, weather fine	MR.

Original

Army Form C. 2118.

WAR DIARY
or
INTELLIGENCE SUMMARY.
(Erase heading not required.)

2/ 4th Duke of Wellingtons Regt

Place	Date	Hour	Summary of Events and Information	Remarks and references to Appendices
Field	11/4/18		Battalion was relieved in the front line by the 2/4th D of W. Regt & proceeded to support line	see also operation order. Appendix
	12/4/18		Weather fine. In support line neighbourhood aeroplanes very active by both artillery	w.t.
	13/4/18		Weather fine. Ordinary trench routine under adverse conditions	w.t.
	14/4/18		Weather dull. Ordinary trench routine. Working parties digging new line	w.t.
	15/4/18		Weather fine. Ordinary trench routine. New line examined.	w.t.
	16/4/18		Battalion was relieved by 2/5th West Yorkshire Regiment & proceeded to the purple line at ESSARTS. (vide Operation Order No 9)	see also operation order appendix 2
	17/4/18		New defensive positions dug. Much material saved	w.t.
	18/4/18		Working parties during the day	"
	19/4/18		New positions improved. Both artillery very active. Much material saved	w.t.
	20/4/18		Same routine.	"

WAR DIARY
or
INTELLIGENCE SUMMARY.
(Erase heading not required.)

Army Form C. 2118.

2/4th Bn. K.R. Duke of Wellingtons Regt.

Place	Date	Hour	Summary of Events and Information	Remarks and references to Appendices
Jus	21/4/18		Weather fine. Hostile artillery very active. Trench mortars and rifle grenades	
	22/4/18		Weather fine. Posts improved	
	23/4/18		Weather fine. Companies working on posts	
	24/4/18		Battalion relieved the line by 1st Essex Regiment proceeded to camp at BOIS-DU-WARNIMONT in accordance with operation order No 20. Weather broke	
BOIS DE WARNIMONT	25/4/18		Battalion in camp cleaning up. Weather splendid	
	26/4/18		Battalion training. Company drill musketry training sniper specialist officers. Weather dull	
	27/4/18		Weather fine. Companies practising ceremonial drill much fast.	
	28/4/18		Battalion proceeded working party on the RED LINE. Weather fine	
	29/4/18		Battalion took part in Brigade tactical exercise all morning. Weather good	

WAR DIARY
or
INTELLIGENCE SUMMARY.

(Erase heading not required.)

2/7 Bn Duke of Wellington's Regt

Army Form C. 2118.

Place	Date	Hour	Summary of Events and Information	Remarks and references to Appendices
BOIS DE WARNIMONT	30/4/18		Weather very bad. Brigade ceremonial parade cancelled owing to state of weather. Lectures in tents. Casualties during month:- Other ranks - 8 killed, 2 died of wounds, 43 wounded, 3 gassed. Honours during month as per Appendix H.	Appx H

F. S. Thackeray... Lt. Colonel
Commanding
2/7th BN. DUKE OF WELLINGTON'S REGT.

2/5th Duke of Wellington's Regt
Operation Order No 20   Copy No 9

Reference Map 57D.    Appendice 3

1. The Battalion will be relieved in Divisional Reserve by the 1st ESSEX Regt on night April 24/25th.

2. Companies will be relieved as under
A Coy 2/7 D of W by W Coy 1st E Regt
B   "   "   "   "   X
C   "   "   "   "   Y
D   "   "   "   "   Z

3. Advance parties of relieving Unit will arrive tonight (April 23/24) at about 9-30 P.M.

4. Platoon guides will report to 2 Lieut Storry at Battalion H.Q at 7 P.M on night of relief and proceed to Rendezvous at track junction E.21.D.9.4. Guides will have written instructions
2 Lieut Storry will be responsible for the correct allotment of these guides

5. If the relieving Unit has only 3 Platoons per Coy the following re-arrangements in dispositions will be made.
   (A) 2 Platoons will take over from 3 in BRADFORD POST
   (B) 2 Platoons will take over from 3 in CONEY TRENCH
   (C) 1 Platoon will take over from 2 in HALIFAX POST
   (D) Only 1 Platoon will be in Reserve in "A" Company's Sector. Guides will be altered in accordance

6. All defence schemes, Trench Maps, and Sketches etc will be handed over.

All Trench Stores will be handed over and positions of dumps made known to relieving Unit.

A list of Stores to be handed over will be forwarded to Battalion H.Q. by 5 P.M. on day of relief.

All work in hand and proposals for work will be carefully handed over

3

7. Completion of relief will be notified to Battalion H.Q. by phrases as under :—
   A Coy — "20 posts arrived"
   B " — "25 Coils wire required"
   C " — "Cannot trace reference"
   D " — "Yet, two wanted"

8. On relief, Battalion will move into billets in the BOIS-DE-WARNIMONT. (T24. A.5.8.)

9. Route will be ESSARTS - HANNESCAMPS - BIENVILLERS - SOUASTRE - Cross Roads D21.B.2.0. Road junction J1.B.0.2. Road junction J1.D.4.7. - ST LEGER - Billets.

10. 100 yards distance between companies and 50 yards between platoons will be maintained.
    When West of the Grid Line between D and E squares, Companies may march as companies.

11. All Trench stores, petrol tins, Blankets etc which can be dispensed with will be stacked at Ration Dump by 4 P.M. Transport Officer will arrange to collect Company Limbers for Lewis

3

Guns etc., will be at E.17 central or the HANNESCAMPS - ESSARTS Road.

12. Hot tea will be provided at about D.21.c.9.7. from thence Rear H.Q. will provide guides to billets.

13. Rear H.Q. are arranging to take over billets.

14. Arrival in billets will be notified to Battalion H.Q.

15. ACKNOWLEDGE

H Ormond
Capt & Adjt
2/7th Bn Duke of Wellington's Regt.

23-4-18.

Copies to :-
1. O.C. 'A' Coy   2. O.C. 'B' Coy
3. O.C. 'C' "   4. O.C. 'D' "
5. 186th Inf Bde.   6. 1st ESSEX Regt.
7. Rear H.Q.   8. Details
9. War Diary   10. File

Advance Copy to —

2/7th Duke of Wellington Regt
Operation Order No 16

(1) The Battalion will be relieved in the line by the 2/4th Bn of W Regt to-morrow-night night 1/2 d April

(2) Companies will be relieved as under
 "A" 2/7th   by "A" 2/4th
 "B"   "   "   "B"   "
 "C"   "   "   "C"   "
 "D"   "   "   "D"   "

(3) Relief will arrive at Serapeum at following times
 B Coy   9 P.M
 C   11 P.M
 D   1 A.M

(4) Platoon guides will be res

by Companies to Rendezvous at F.21.b.9.6. (Ration Dump) at following times.

  B Coy 8. PM
  C "   10. PM
  D "   12 Midnight

They will there report to an Officer of 'A' Coy who will be responsible for their correct allotment.

(5) O.C 'A' Coy will arrange direct with O.C 'B' Coy 2/4 D of W to carry out his relief during the evening.
This relief can be carried out in daylight with no movement over the open.

(6) Advance party of 1 Officer per Company will report Companies on night 10/11th

(7) Completion of relief will be

reported by phrase "Lewis Gun course 'L'" followed by name of Coy Commander.

(8) On relief Companies will move into positions vacated by Companies of 2/4 D of W as under.
Position vacated by A Coy/fs by D Coy
    "   "   B   "   A "
    "   "   C   "   B "
    "   "   D   "   C "

(9) Guides of 2/4th for these positions will be picked up at the ration dump F.21.b.9.6.

(10) One Officer and 1 runner per Company will report at Batt H2 by 5 AM on 11th April to proceed to reconnoitre 2/4 positions.

(11) Arrival in new position will be notified by phrase "Name for Leave '—'" followed by the name of Company 2nd i/c

(12) All Trench Stores, defence schemes etc will be carefully handed and take over.

/Sd/ H Ormerod. Capt
                                Adjt
2/7th Bn Duke of Wellington's Regt
10.4.18.

Copies to (1) OC Companies
            (2) 2/4th D of W
            (3) File
            (4) War Diary

2/7th Duke of Wellington's Regt
Operation Order No 17.

(I) Operation Order No 16 is postponed for one night.

(II) Following Relief will take place tonight.
(a) 'B' Coy will extend their line and take over from the two left Platoons of 'D' Coy 5th West Ridings immediately on their right.
(b) To help this 2Lt H.W.Smith will take over with his platoon from left front platoon of 'B' Coy 2/7th D of W Regt. Arrangements for above relief will be made by O.C. Coy concerned.

III 'A' Coy 2/7th D of W Regt will relieve the two Right Platoons of 'D' Coy 5th West Ridings and two platoons of 'B' Coy 5th West Ridings (Centre Company) from F.23.c.0.3. approx to F.28.b.8.7. approx. Guides for 'A' Coy will be at BHQ at 8.30 P.M.

IV 'D' Coy 2/7th D of W will be relieved by Bn on our left and on relief will move into Bn reserve into positions vacated by 'A' Coy.

V Ration Dump tonight will be as usual.

VI Completion of relief will be reported by phrase "Lewis Gun Course" followed by name of Coy Commander.

VII Usual receipts for Trench Stores will be given and receipts

obtained and Lists forwarded to
Bn HQ by 10 AM. 12.4.18.

VIII Acknowledge by wire.

11.4.18
           H Drinnod. Capt & Adjt
2/7th Bn Duke of Wellington's Regt

Copies to :-
1   O b Coys.
2   2/Lieut W Smith M.M.
3   File
4   War Diary
5   5th West Riding Regt

2/7th Bn Duke of Wellington's Regt

Operation Orders No 18.

I Operation Order No 16 is cancelled and the following relief substituted on night 12/13th inst.

II Left Coy 'D' Coy 2/4 will relieve 'C' Coy 2/7th
   Centre - 'C' - 2/4 - - 'B' - 2/7th
   Right - 'A' - 2/4 - - 'A' - 2/7th
   Reserve - 'B' - 2/4 - - 'D' - 2/7th

III Platoon Guides will report to 2/Lt Greenhow of 'D' Coy at Bridge at F.21.b.9.6. at the following hours.
   'A' Coy 2/7th   at   8.30 P.M.
   'C' - 2/7th   at   10.30 P.M.
   'B' - 2/7th   at   12.30 P.M.
'D' Coy 2/7th D of W will not provide guides but will report to 'B' Coy 2/4th when vacating their present position vide para VI.

IV 'A' Coy 2/7th will arrange to provide 2 Guides at Ration dump at Bridge at F.21.b.9.6. to bring up Ration party of 'A' Coy 2/4th at 9 P.M.

V On relief Companies will be located as follows.

'A' Coy 2/7th with 2 Platoons in F.21.c
                 2 Platoons in F.27.b.
with Coy HQ at F.21.c.
replacing 'A' Coy 2/4th D of W Regt

'B' Coy 2/7th in F.20.d. replacing 'C' Coy 2/4
'C' - 2/7th in F.21.d. - - D -
'D' - 2/7th in Road in F.22.a and c.
replacing 'A' Coy 5th West Riding Regt

VI. 'D' Coy 4th will move into their new position on vacation of same by 5th West Riding Regt establishing their Coy HQ at F.32.c.1.3.
This move will not take place before dusk.

VII. Completion of relief will be reported to Bn HQ by the phrase — "No socks required" followed by name of O.C. Coy.

VIII. (a) On relief 'A' 'C' and 'B' Coys will move to the ration dump at Bridge at F.21.b.9.6. and will pick up guides and rations and move into new positions.
(b) O.C. 'D' Coy will arrange for his own guides and will draw rations after arrival in new position.

IX. O.C. 'D' Coy 4th will arrange to reconnoitre his new position immediately.

X. Arrival in new position will be reported by phrase — "Name for Leave" — followed by name of CSM (to new Bn HQ)

XI. Usual receipts for stores etc will be given and received

XII. Bn HQ on completion of relief will be at F.21.d.1.6.

XIII. 'A' 'C' and 'B' Coys will send an advance party of 1 Offr and 1 ORR about 11 pm to take over dispositions, stores and work in hand.

Acknowledge.

12.4.18.

H Ormerod. Capt & Adjt
2/7th Bn Duke of Wellington's Regt

Copies to :-

1. O.B. Coys.
2. 5th West Riding Regt.
3. 2/4th Duke of Wellington's Regt
4. War Diary
5. File.

Appendix I   Copy No 2
2/7 Duke of Wellington's Regt.
Operation Order No 19

(1) The battalion will be relieved in reserve by 2/5 West YORKSHIRE Regt to-night April 17th/18th

(2) Companies will be relieved alphabetically ie A Coy 2/7 by A Coy 2/5 W.Y. and so-on

(3) Platoon guides will be sent to Cross roads F.20.b.00.95 to rendezvous there at 9.30 p.m.
An N.C.O. will be sent with each company's guides and he will have written instructions.

(4) Advance parties of relieving unit will report to their respective companies this afternoon.

(5) All petrol tins, dirty socks, etc which are to go to Wagon Lines will be dumped at the present ration dump as companies are relieved. OC 'D' Coy will arrange to send his tins etc to the main battalion ration dump during the evening. Transport Officer will arrange to collect.

(6) Completion of relief will be reported by the phrase "no more wine required"

(7) On relief companies will take over from the same companies that relieved them in the line and will /be

be in Divisional Reserve.

(8) ~~Bn~~ Company HQ will be as follows
    A Coy   E 24 d 7.8
    B Coy   E 24 d 5.2
    C Coy   E 19 a 3.0
    D Coy   E 24 a 8.7
Battalion HQ   E 24 d 7.8

(9) Arrival in new positions will be reported by phrase "Rations at usual time".

(10) All Trench stores, defence schemes, maps etc will be carefully handed over & taken over.
All work in hand will have particular attention given to it

(11) Rations to night will be dumped by transport at dumps taken over from 2/5 W.Y. and companies will collect immediately on arrival

(3) Acknowledge
        H Cromwell Capt & adj
        2/4 Duke of Wellington's

17.4.18
   Copies to
   (1) to (4) OC Coys
   (5) 2/5 West Yorks
   (6) Details
   (7) File
   (8) War Diary

APPENDIX IV.

HONOURS.

By Commander of IV Corps, under authority delegated to him.

MILITARY MEDAL.

306659 Pte L. Hainsworth.   (attach'd 186th. Inf. Bde).
267177 L/C Hay A.
305907 Cpl Blakeley J.E.

(Authority D.R.O. 1281 of 22.4.18.).

By Commander of IV Corps, under authority delegated to him.

BAR TO MILITARY MEDAL.

26695 Cpl R. Nutter, M.M.   'B' Coy.
266932 Pte W. Smales, M.M.   'B' Coy.

MILITARY MEDAL.

10926 L/C J. Holmes.   'A' Coy.
305283 Pte H.B. Fisher.   'A' Coy.

(Authority :- D.R.O. 1287 of 26.4.18.).

SECRET

War Diary
— of —
2/4th Bn. Duke of Wellington's (W.R) Regt.

From:- 1.5.18
To:- 31.5.18.

Rendered in accordance with
F.S. Regulations Part II.

F. Shuttleworth
Lieut Colonel
Comg.
2/4th. Duke of Wellington's Regiment

WAR DIARY
or
INTELLIGENCE SUMMARY.

(Erase heading not required.)

ORIGINAL   Army Form C. 2118.

2/7 DUKE OF WELLINGTONS
(W.R.) REGT.

Instructions regarding War Diaries and Intelligence Summaries are contained in F.S. Regs., Part II. and the Staff Manual respectively. Title pages will be prepared in manuscript.

Place	Date	Hour	Summary of Events and Information	Remarks and references to Appendices
BOIS DE WARLIMONT	1/5/18		A. B. C. Coys carried out a tactical exercise. D. Coy musketry etc.	Sgt.
	2/5/18		2 Lieut. T. Gold joined the Bett.	
			Battalion took part in Brigade Pinshaw attack	Sgt.
			The C.R.E gave a lecture on "Organisation of Working Parties"	
	3/5/18		The Battalion was at work on the "RED LINE"	Sgt.
	4/5/18		— do — do — do —	Sgt.
	5/5/18		— do — do — do —	Sgt.
	6/5/18		The Battalion worked on the PURPLE LINE	Sgt.
	7/5/18		The Battalion attended Div. Natior. ADTHE Coy. training.	Sgt.
	8/5/18		Decorations were awarded by the Divn Commander the Officers N.C.O + Men 7th Brigade. 2/7 D.G.W. 296. 2/4 D.G.W. 296.	Sgt.
			Football Result. 2/7 D.G.W. 296. 2/4 D.G.W. 296.	
	9/5/18		Coys practised the attack	Sgt.
	10/5/18		Coy training	Sgt.
	11/5/18		Battalion Sports were held Football Result. 62 M.G.C. v qd. 2/7 D.G.W. 196	Sgt.

WAR DIARY or INTELLIGENCE SUMMARY

Army Form C. 2118. ORIGINAL

2/4 DUKE DE WELLINGTON'S (W.R.) REGT

Place	Date	Hour	Summary of Events and Information	Remarks and references to Appendices
BOIS DE WARLEMONT	12/5/16		The Battalion attended Divine Service. Foothill Result. 2/4 D.A.W. 3qbs 2/4 D.A.W. M4	SWY
	13/5/16		The Battalion prepared the attack	SWY
	14/5/16		The Battalion finished the attack. Foothill Result 1/9 Durham L.I. 2qbs 2/7/9 W.I	SWY
	15/5/16		The Div Gas Officer lectured the Batt on Gas. The day was spent in making final preparations for the line. Foothill Result. 2/4 D.G.W. 2qbs 62 M.G.C. MG During the pack period of training, The Batt Band gave in series of Concerts. The Div. Concert Party "The Pelicans" also gave a few other an Concerts.	SWY
	16/5/16		At 5.30 PM the Batt left BOIS DE WARLEMONT & proceeded in Motor Lorries to SOOASTRE. Here it relieved the 8 LINCOLN REGT in the BUSNOY SECTOR during the night. The Batt proceeded via BIENVILLES & ESSARTS to the line. 2 Lt C. Scott was wounded in the face just after leaving SOUASTRE. The Batt relieved the 8 LINCOLN REGT in the BUSNOY SECTOR during the night 2/4 D. OF. W. Batt is the Left Brigade. (SYDNE.)	Appendices
S-T-D NE	17/5/16		On our Left 2/4 WEST YORKS & on our Right 2/4 D. OF W. The weather was extremely fine & the enemy was very quiet. A man was	SWY
	18/5/16		Captured by B.Coy belonging to the 164 IR 111 Div.	SWY

Army Form C. 2118.

ORIGINAL

WAR DIARY
or
INTELLIGENCE SUMMARY.
(Erase heading not required.)

2/4 DUKE OF WELLINGTONS (W.R.) REGT.

Instructions regarding War Diaries and Intelligence Summaries are contained in F.S. Regs., Part II. and the Staff Manual respectively. Title pages will be prepared in manuscript.

Place	Date	Hour	Summary of Events and Information	Remarks and references to Appendices
LINE 51D NE	18/5/18	6 A.M.	A party of the enemy were seen & engaged in BOCQUOY CEMETERY. The enemy fled leaving one man killed. He belonged to the 164 I.R. III Div. Enemy quiet. Weather fine.	S.W.
	19/5/18		Enemy Artillery active on our supports. Our patrols active. The Work in hand was carried on.	S.W.
	20/5/18		Enemy Artillery still very active. The enemy sent up a great number of Very lights during the night.	S.W.
	21/5/18		Enemy Artillery less active. A good deal of transport heard during the night.	S.W.
	22/5/18		Enemy Artillery extremely quiet. Much movement was seen during the day. The weather was still extremely hot & no Aeroplanes took advantage of the fine spell.	S.W.
	23/5/18		Enemy rather active with T.Ms. During the afternoon 8th Hussars in our right Coy sector. The enemy swept our positions with 77 M.M, 105 M.M & 150 M.M guns. There was considerable Arcot activity during the night.	W.
	24/5/18		Very quiet. The Bn was relieved by the 2/4 D. of N. & went into support.	Appendix 2
	25/5/18		Very quiet. A great Aerial fight 670ft was done in the trenches	M.T.

WAR DIARY
or
INTELLIGENCE SUMMARY.

(Erase heading not required.) 2/4 DUKE OF WELLINGTON'S (W.R.) REGT.

Army Form C. 2118.

ORIGINAL

Place	Date	Hour	Summary of Events and Information	Remarks and references to Appendices
LINE 54 NE	26/5/18		Enemy Artillery very active in our rear. Weather still fine	5x1
	27/5/18		— do — do —	5x1.
	28/5/18		At 1AM BICOUSE CEMETERY was raided by "A" Coy. No identifications were obtained. Very quiet during the day.	Appendix 5x1
	29/5/18		Very quiet. Weather still very fine. RIDING REGT in the left sector. The Batt. relieved the 5 WEST	Appendix 5x1
	30/5/18		1st GRENADIER GUARDS on our left. 2/4 Down on our right. Very quiet	a.y.
	31/5/18		Very quiet. Weather still very fine	v.y.

1.6.18

F.S. Halsey ?Col
Comdg 2/4 D.L. of Wellington Regt

Appendix 1

Copy No. 9........

2/7th. BN. DUKE OF WELLINGTON'S REGIMENT.

OPERATION ORDER NO. 22.

1. The Battalion will relieve the 8th. Bn. Lincolnshire Regiment in the line to-morrow night, the 16/17th. instant.

2. Companies will relieve as under :-
   'B' Coy. 2/7th.Bn. Right Forward Coy. relieving 'A' Coy.8th.L.R.
   'A' "   "   "   Left   "   "   "   'B' "   "   "
   'C' "   "   "   Right Support Coy.   "   'C' "   "   "
   'D' "   "   "   Left   "   "   "   'D' "   "   "

3. The Battalion will proceed via SOUASTRE - BIENVILLERS - HANNESCAMPS - ESSART - FRONT LINE.
   DRESS :- Fighting Order.

4. Platoon Guides will meet the Battalion at the old British front line at E.17.a.6.4. about 8.45 p.m.
   Dispositions are as already circulated.
   All movement East of SOUASTRE will be by Platoons at not less than 150 yards distance.

5. Advance Parties, as already detailed, will proceed to the line to-night by Motor Lorry leaving AUTHIE at 7.0 p.m.
   They will be met by Guides at E.17.a.6.4. at 9.0 p.m.

6. All Trench Stores, Maps, Aeroplane Photographs, will be taken over and lists forwarded to Battalion Headquarters as soon as possible. All work in hand and details of proposed work will also be carefully taken over.

7. Completion of relief will be reported to Battalion Headquarters by code phrases as under :-
   'A' Coy. "No vacancies required."
   'B' Coy. "Lewis Gun Course cancelled."
   'C' Coy. "30 Colts required."
   'D' Coy. "R.E.Indent - nil."

8. Os.C.Companies will make the necessary arrangements for cooking in accordance with the instructions already circulated.

9. Eight partially trained Lewis Gunners per Company, as detailed by the Lewis Gun Officer, will remain out of the line to undergo a Brigade Course assembling at ORVILLE. Orders for the move of this party will be issued later.
   The four Reserve Guns will be transported with this party. Transport Officer will arrange.
   The Cook Sergeant will make arrangements to send 2 Dixies, 1 Ladle and 1 Felling Axe to the Brigade School.

10. No nucleus personnel will be left out of the line.

11. Hot tea will be provided under arrangements made by the Cook Sergeant on the SOUASTRE - BIENVILLERS Road.
    Company Limbers will report to Companies at this point.

1.

12. All packs, blankets, surplus stores, etc. will be stacked at the Quartermaster's Stores by 12 noon to-morrow. The Transport Officer will arrange to transport these to the new Wagon Lines.

13. The Camp will be handed over by the Quartermaster to a Representative of the 8th. Bn. Lincolnshire Regiment and receipt and clearing certificate obtained. These will be forwarded to Orderly Room.

14. Rear Headquarters will detail the personnel mentioned in paras. 19 and 20 of Administrative Instructions already issued.

H Ormerod
Captain & Adjutant,
5/7th. Bn. Duke of Wellington's Regiment.

Time of Issue 5.0 p.m.

Copies to :-

No. 1. O.C. 'A' Coy.
No. 2. O.C. 'B' Coy.
No. 3. O.C. 'C' Coy.
No. 4. O.C. 'D' Coy.
No. 5. Rear Headquarters.
No. 6. 8th. Bn. Lincolnshire Regt.
No. 7. Details.
No. 8. File.
No. 9. War Diary.

Amendment to Para. 12. Packs and blankets will be stacked by 9.0 a.m. Surplus Stores by 12 noon.

Appx. to 13.

2/4 Duke of [...] [...]
Operation order [...] Appendix

(1) The battalion will be [relieved] in the
line by the [...] on the night 24/[...] [...]
by the 2/4 Duke of [Wellington's] Regt.

(2) Companies will be relieved as follows:
  C # Coy by D Coy
  D   "   A
  B   C
  A   B

(3) 1 Guide per platoon [...] for Coy HQ to
  rendezvous as under:
  A & B Coys at junction of trench
  & road at OF 21 c 8.4 at 11 pm
  C and D Coys at junction of trench
  & road at IT 20 a 6.5 at 10 PM.
  O/C 'A' Coy will detail an officer
  to take charge of A & B Coy
  guides. O/C 'C' Coy will detail an
  officer for C & D Coy guides.
  Guides will have written instructions.
  These routes should be reconnoitred
  during daylight.

(4) An advance party of 1 officer and
  4 N.C.O's per Coy will report tonight

To Companies   Copy. No 18

(5) All Trench Stores etc will be carefully
handed over. A list of these will
be forwarded to Regt HQ
by 4 PM tomorrow

(6) Completion of relief will be reported
to HQ as under
  A Coy   "Salvage hut"
  B   "
  C   Sick billet ?
  D   S/O ? post ? wanted

(7) On relief the Batt will have this
support position relieved by 2/4
Batt D. of W. Regt and companies
will take over from the Companies
that relieves them in the line

(8) An advance party of 1 officer +
4 NCO's per Coy will be sent to
HQ 2/4 D. of W. Regt [F.21. c 4 6] ?
at 10 AM 24 inst. This party will
act as guides for Company at night
and will rendezvous at any point
to be selected by OC Company
concerned.

A list of stores [?] taken over will be forwarded to HQ 2/a/c soon as possible.

10. Arrival at new posts [?] will be notified by following code phrases:-
    A Coy — Send up ration
    B " — Tea rum sugar [?]
    C " — No [?] sugar [?]
    D " — [?]

11. During relief [Coy's] may use any convenient route.

12. Ration Dumps to-morrow will be as taken over from the 2/4 [?] of W. Regt. All petrol tins will be taken by Companies to Read dumps.

13. Acknowledge — [illegible]
                                    Capt & Adj
    23.5.18   2/1(?) of W. Regt.

                Copies to
    1/ "A" Coy   2/ "B" Coy   3/ "C" Coy
    4/ D Coy   5/ 186 Inf Bde 6/ 2/4 [?] of W. Regt
    7/ [?] W.R.   8/ 2/7 West Yorks 9/ MGC
    10/ TMB   11/ Rear HQ   12/ [?]
    13/ War Diary 14/ file

Copy No. 14

2/7th BN. DUKE OF WELLINGTON'S REGIMENT.

Operation Order No 26.

----oooOooo----

1. The Battalion will relieve the 5th Bn West Riding Regt in the line on the night 29/30th May.

2. On completion of relief Companies will be disposed as under :-

    'D' Company   Right Front.
    'B'   "   Left Front.
    'A'   "   Right Support.
    'C'   "   Left Support.

3. Companies will relieve Companies of 5th Bn West Riding Regt as under :-

    'D' Company 2/7th   will relieve   'D' Company 5th W.R.Regt.
    'B'   "   "   "   "   'A'   "   "   "
    'A'   "   "   "   "   'B'   "   "   "
    'C'   "   "   "   "   'C'   "   "   "

4. An advance party of 1 Officer per Company and 1 N.C.O. per platoon will report to Headquarters 5th Bn West Riding Regt at 12 midnight 28/29th May.

5. One platoon from 'A' Company will be attached to 'D' Company, and one from 'C' Company to 'B' Company. These platoons will report to their respective Companies 1 hour before relief commences and will come under these Companies for Tactics, Discipline and Rations.

6. Guides will not be provided for 'C' Company who will move from present position at 9 p.m. Platoon guides will meet Companies at junction of TOP TRENCH and PRUSSIAN AVENUE (F.21.c.7.2) at following times :-

    'A' Company (less one platoon)   9.30 p.m.
    'D'   "   (plus one platoon)   10 p.m.
    'B'   "   (plus one platoon)   10.30 p.m.

7. All trench stores, maps, defence schemes etc will be carefully taken over and lists of such stores forwarded to Battalion H.Q. as soon as possible.

8. Completion of relief will be reported to Battn H.Q. by following Code Phrases :-

    'A' Company   "Have rations arrived"
    'B'   "   "Screw pickets required"
    'C'   "   "Bi-carbonate received".
    'D'   "   "Is wire available".

9. Companies of 5th Bn West Riding Regt will move into positions vacated by the Companies relieving them in the line.

10. An advance party of 5th Bn West Riding Regt will report to Companies on the morning of 29th inst. No guides will be required from this Unit.

11. A list of trench stores to be handed over in present positions will be forwarded to H.Q. by 4 p.m. 29th inst.

-1-

12. Ration dumps and arrangements will be as taken over from the 5th Bn West Riding Regt. Rations will arrive at Dumps on night of relief about 1.15 a.m. All petrol tins etc to go down the line on night of relief will be dumped at 'C' Company's present Ration Dump before relief commences.

ACKNOWLEDGE.

Capt. & Adjutant
2/7th Bn Duke of Wellington's Regiment.

28.5.1918.

Copies to :-
1. 'A' Coy.
2. 'B'
3. 'C'
4. 'D'
5. 186th Inf.Bde.
6. 5th Bn W.R.Regt.
7. 2/4th Bn D of W's Regt.
8. Left flank Bn.
9. M.G.C.
10. 186th T.M.B.
11. Rear H.Q.
12. Details.
13. File.
14. War Diary.

Secret   Copy No. 14.

2/7TH BN. DUKE OF WELLINGTON'S REGIMENT   Appendix 4

Operation Order No 25.
-----oOo-----

1. 'A' Company under Capt G.J.H.Miller., M.C. (O.C. Enterprise)
    will carry out a "Stealth Raid" on the night of 27/28th
    May against BUCQUOY CEMETERY with the object of obtaining
    identifications and causing loss to the enemy.

Composition   Four Raiding parties. A.B.C and D of 1 N.C.O and 6 men, each
of Parties.   to work in pairs. A and B under 2/Lieut A.B.Smith,
   2.   C and D under Lieut J.H.Charlesworth.
              Two Sappers with a Bangalore Torpedo will accompany each of
              these two parties.
              A Lewis Gun Party E to act as a left flank guard and to cover
              the advance of A.B.C and D parties should it be necessary.
              1 N.C.O and 6 men including Rifle Bombers with Nos 24 and 27
              (smoke) grenades, accompanied by four stretcher-bearers.
              A Reserve Platoon D with two Lewis Guns and Rifle Bombers
              armed with No 3. grenades, to act as required under O.C.
              Enterprise, accompanied by 8 stretcher-bearers.
                 Note : Section organisation to be retained.

Action of   Lewis Gun Party E will be pushed out first to about
Parties.   L.4.a.80.75. Raiding parties A.B.C and D will follow
   3.   moving out from the hedge in front of Post No 7 (F.25.c.5.0)
              close up to hedge for a distance of about 100 yards when
              they will extend their front as they advance so that C and D
              parties enter the CEMETERY to the East of the dividing hedge
              L.4.a.5.7.
              A and B parties to work on either side of hedge which runs
              from F.25.c.5.0. to L.4.a.5.7.
              Should gaps which have been reported to exist in CEMETERY
              hedge prove to have been blocked, the Bangalore Torpedoes
              will be used.
              On entering CEMETERY, parties will wheel to their left and
              clear their portion of it, ensuring that the whole CEMETERY
              has been mopped up.
              These parties will withdraw 10 minutes after entering by
              the same route by which they entered (or if this is
              impossible towards Post No 5.

              The Lewis Gun party E will be prepared to neutralize any
              M.G. fire from the direction of the CRUCIFIX by Lewis Gun
              fire and Rifle Grenade fire (including smoke grenades).
              They must be careful not to fire to the West of this point
              when Raiding parties are in the CEMETERY.
              The Reserve Platoon will move out after the Raiding parties
              to a position about L.4.a.0.5.
              Withdrawal will take place in the following order :-

                 (1) Raiding parties A.B.C and D.
                 (2) Lewis Gun Party E.
                 (3) Reserve Platoon.

              Should it be necessary for Raiding parties to withdraw
              direct to Nos 4,5, or 6 Posts, Red Very Lights will be
              fired from these posts to correspond with the number of
              parties returned there.
              Party Leaders will ensure that no men of their party is
              left behind for any purpose whatever. The chain of
              command will be made known to all men of each party.
              The signal for Raiding parties to move forward will be the
              13th shot fired by the Stokes Mortars as below :-

Stokes Mortars. Three Stokes Mortars will be specially placed to fire
   4.   into CEMETERY and at Machine Guns East of CEMETERY prior to
              the assault. They will each fire 6 rounds.
              The Stokes Mortars will commence firing at Zero.

Artillery.   18 pounders will open at a slow rate of fire at
5.   Zero plus 2" for 10 minutes on present S.O.S. line
                    of D/293 Battery and on line L.3.d.3.2. to L.4.c.4.7.
                    to detract attention.

Communication.   O.C. Raid will make his Headquarters at No 8 Post
6.   in close touch with the Reserve Platoon.
                    A lamp will be established at this point to signal to
                    an advanced Battalion Station in Hedge trench.
                    DD messages will be used.

Dress and equipment. Dress :-   Service Dress, Caps S.D. (all identificat-
7.   ions removed). Raiding identity discs.

A.B.C and D Parties.

Every man :- Rifle and bayonet (blackened).
Four pairs wire-cutters.
Every other man :- No 23 cup attachment and three
Rifle Grenades.

Party E.

1 Lewis Gun.
24 Drums.
50 rounds per man.
36 Rifle Bombs (No 24.)
1 Stretcher.
12 Smoke bombs (No 27) Rifle.

Reserve Platoon.

2 Lewis Guns, with 24 drums each.
8 Dischargers (No 36)
48 Rifle Bombs (No 36)
3 Stretchers.
8 Wire-cutters.

Watches will be synchronised at Headquarters 2/7th Bn
Duke of Wellington's Regt at 4 p.m. 27th inst.

A Report Centre will be established at Headquarters 2/4th
Bn Duke of Wellington's Regt during Raid, where all
messages will be sent.

Zero hour will be 1.50 a.m.

O.C. Signals will arrange to send two trained signallers with the
Reserve Platoon and they will take a Lucas Lamp. They will get in
touch with the Post to be established in HEDGE Trench. Bearings and
map references will be issued to O.C. Signals separately.

O.C. 'B' Company will detail three N.C.O's and three men to fire the
red signals mentioned in para 3. This party will report to Capt
G.W.M.Miller.,M.C. at 2 p.m. 27th inst for instructions.
O.C. 'B' Company will also detail two runners who know the location of
No 3A Post, Left Company Frontage, Right Battalion Section, Left Sub-
Section. They will report to Capt G.W.M.Miller.,M.C. at 2 p.m. 27th
inst for instructions.

Stretcher-bearers as under will report to O.C. Enterprise at 10 p.m.
27th inst.

   One squad Headquarters complete with stretchers and bag of
   shell dressings.
   One squad (Two men 'C' Company, two men 'D' Company) complete
   with stretchers and bag of shell dressings as detailed by
   Medical Officer.

Hot food will be issued to Raiding party under arrangements with
O.C. 'B' Company before Raid. Tea will be issued after the Raid.

All N.C.O's in charge of Parties or individuals who may become detached will report to Battalion Headquarters as soon as possible for checking casualties.

                                                        Capt & Adjt
                              2/7th Bn Duke of Wellington's Regiment.

27.5.1918.

Copies to :-

1. O.C. 'A' Company.
2. Lieut J.H.Charlesworth.
3. 2/Lieut A.B.Smith.
4. 186th Infantry Brigade.
5. 5th Bn West Riding Regiment.
6. Right Battalion.
7. 2/4th Bn Duke of Wellington's Regiment.
8. 186th T.M.Battery.
9. Right Group Artillery.
10. M.G.C.
11. 461 Field Coy R.E.
12. 6" T.M.Battery.
13. Rear Headquarters.
14. Details. i.e.   'B' Company.
                  'C'   "
                  'D'   "
                Medical Officer.
15. File.
16. War Diary.

SECRET.

186 Original
7/N/18
Ceased

War Diary

2/7th Bn. Duke of Wellington's Regiment

From :- June 1st. 1918.
To :- June 18th 1918.

Volume XVIII.

Rendered in accordance with F.S. Regulations

Part II

2/6 DUKE OF
WELLINGTONS

WAR DIARY

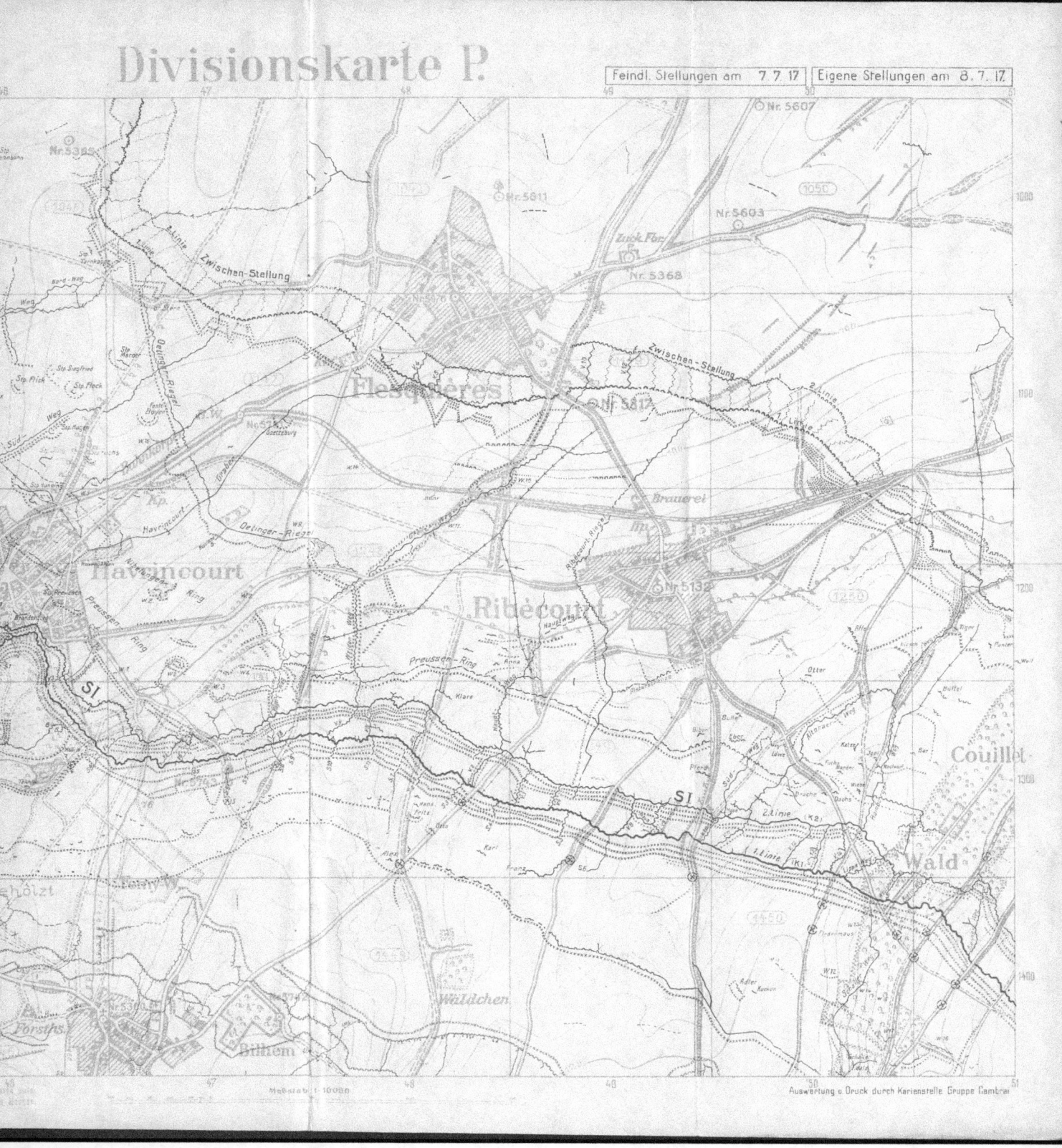

2/6 DUKE OF WELLINGTONS

WAR DIARY

(CAPTURED MAP)

SECRET

War Diary

2/7th Bn. Duke of Wellington's Regiment

From :- June 1st. 1918.
To :- June 18th 1918.

Volume XVIII.

Rendered in accordance with F.S. Regulations

Part II

186 Original
62/9/51/18
Censed

F. Beaumont
Major.
Commanding
2/7th Bn Duke of Wellington's Regiment

1.7.1918.

Army Form C. 2118.

WAR DIARY
or
INTELLIGENCE SUMMARY.

2/4 DUKE OF WELLINGTONS (W.R.) REGT

ORIGINAL

Instructions regarding War Diaries and Intelligence Summaries are contained in F.S. Regs., Part II. and the Staff Manual respectively. Title pages will be prepared in manuscript.

(Erase heading not required.)

Place	Date	Hour	Summary of Events and Information	Remarks and references to Appendices
MAP SHEET NE ABLAINZEVELLE LINE	1/6/18		Very quiet during the day. At night enemy shelled ground in our rear with Gas Shells for an hour. The wind carried the gas into our positions & S.B.R's were worn for a considerable time. Phosgene Gas was used.	S.W.?
	2/6/18		Lieut G. Clifton rejoined the Batt. Very quiet. Weather still fine.	Sw.t
			The Batt was relieved by the 8 WEST YORKSHIRE REGT & moved into the PURPLE SYSTEM. ESSARTS. (appendix 1)	S.W.
			2/Lieut J.W. Pepper M.C. rejoined the Batt.	S.W.t
ESSARTS	3/6/18		Work was carried on in accordance with defence scheme	
	4/6/18		do — do — do —	Sw.t
	5/6/18		do — do — do —	Sw.t
	6/6/18		— do — do — do —	Sw.t
			The Batt was relieved by the 2/4 DUKE OF WELLINGTONS & moved to SOUASTRE (appendix 2)	S.W.
SOUASTRE	7/6/18		The day was spent in cleaning up. Kit inspections were held. The Div Concert Party "The Pelicans" gave a concert at 5.30 p.m.	Sw.t
	8/6/18		The Batt paraded under the R.S.M. for drill in the morning. The Batt turned the Div Baths in the afternoon.	Sw.t
			The Commander of the IV Corps awarded the MILITARY MEDAL to the following N.C.O's & men for gallantry & devotion to duty during operations which commenced March 25th 1918.	Sw.t

WAR DIARY
INTELLIGENCE SUMMARY

2/4 DUKE OF WELLINGTONS (W.R) REGT.

Army Form C. 2118.

Place	Date	Hour	Summary of Events and Information	Remarks and references to Appendices
SOUASTRE	8/6/18 cont		306015 Cpl Baxter J. 23698 Pte Wilson A. 306890 Pte Bancroft J. 308112 Pte Armitage W. 266285 Sgt Golding G. Casualties from 17/5/18 to date were as follows. 7 killed. 2 accidentally killed. 21 Wounded.	Sgt.
	9/6/18		The Batt. attended Divine Service	Sgt.
	10/6/18		The Batt. relieved the 5" K.O.Y.L.I. in the line. (Appendix 3.)	Sgt.
	11/6/18		Very quiet. Weather very good.	Sgt.
	12/6/18		Very quiet. A number of Officers N.C.Os of the 2/4 HAMPSHIRE REGT. being attached for instruction. Casualties 2 killed 1 wounded.	Sgt.
	13/6/18		Very quiet.	Sgt.
	14/6/18		The Batt. was relieved by the 2/4 DUKE OF WELLINGTONS & went into support. (Appendix 4.) 1 killed 4 wounded.	Sgt.
	15/6/18		The Batt. was relieved by the 2/4 HAMPSHIRE REGT. (Appendix 5) & proceeded to SOUASTRE. Then was finally here by 5 DUKE OF WELLINGTONS. Officers the Batt. was conveyed to AMPLIER in buses via HENU & PAS.	Sgt.

Army Form C. 2118.

WAR DIARY
or
INTELLIGENCE SUMMARY.

2/7 DUKE OF WELLINGTONS (W.R.) REGT.

ORIGINAL

(Erase heading not required.)

Place	Date	Hour	Summary of Events and Information	Remarks and references to Appendices
AMPLIER	16/6/18		The Brig Commander bid farewell to the Batt & thanked all ranks for their past service.	
	17/6/18		The C.O. & certain officers & N.C.O.s left for England	
			Parties of Officers, N.C.O.s & men were posted to the 5th & 2/4th Duke of Wellington Regt	
	18/6/18		The remainder of the Batt. was sent to the Base.	

G. Beaumont. Major
Commanding
2/7th Bn Duke of Wellington's Regt.

30.6.1918.

Appendix 1
Copy No. 14

2/7th Bn. DUKE OF WELLINGTON'S REGIMENT.

Operation Orders No 27.

-----ooOoo-----

The Battalion will be relieved in the line on night 2/3rd June by the 8th Bn. West Yorkshire Regt.

Companies will be relieved as under :-
'A' Company 2/7th DofW's by 'A' Company 8th Bn W.Yks Regt.
'B'   "   "   by 'C'   "   "
'C'   "   "   by 'D'   "   "
'D'   "   "   by 'B'   "   "

'A' and 'B' Companies will provide 6 guides and 'A' and 'C' Companies 6 guides who will rendezvous at Cross roads K.14.A.O.C. at 10 p.m. Guides will have written instructions.
2/Lieut N.J.Marsh will be in charge of these guides who will first rendezvous at Battalion H.Q. at 9.15 p.m.
Order of Relief will be 'D' Coy, 'B' Coy, 'C' Coy, 'A' Coy, and H.Q. Coy. Two guides will be provided for H.Q.

An advance party of 1 Officer per Company and 1 N.C.O per platoon will report to forward Companies to-night.
Advance parties for support Companies will report at 7.30 p.m. to-morrow.

All trench stores, defence schemes, aeroplane photographs and work in hand will be carefully handed over. A list of trench Stores to be handed over will be forwarded to H.Q. before noon to-morrow.

Completion of relief will be reported to Battalion H.Q. by following code phrases :-
'A' Company   -   "Send more water".
'B'   "   -   "Tins were all returned".
'C'   "   -   "Send up LYDDI".
'D'   "   -   "Have you a map".

On Completion of relief the Battalion will take over positions vacated by 8th Bn West Yorkshire Regt in Divisional Reserve.

Companies will take over from the 8th Bn West Yorkshire Regt as under :-
'A' Company 2/7th DofW's Regt from 'B' Company 8th West Yks Regt.
'B'   "   "   "   from 'A'   "   "
'C'   "   "   "   from 'C'   "   "
'D'   "   "   "   from 'D'   "   "

An advance party of 1 Officer and 4 N.C.O's per Company will proceed to take over on the morning of June 2nd.
'D' Company's party will be accommodated by 'C' Company for to-night.

The party detailed in para 9. will act as guides for Companies, to rendezvous at a place decided by O's C Companies.

The platoons of 'A' and 'C' Companies attached to 'D' and 'B' Companies will rejoin their Companies in new positions.
Advance parties and guides should be arranged accordingly.

All trench stores, maps and work in hand will be carefully taken over. Lists will be forwarded to Battalion H.Q. as early as possible.

-1-

13. Arrival in new positions will be notified to Battalion H.Q. in BAB Code.

14. Ration arrangements and dumps will be taken over. On June 3rd rations will arrive about 1.15 a.m.

15. ACKNOWLEDGE.

H Ormerod
Capt & Adjutant
2/7th Bn Duke of Wellington's Regiment.

1.6.1918.

Copies to :-

1. O.C. 'A' Company.
2. O.C. 'B'   "
3. O.C. 'C'   "
4. O.C. 'D'   "
5. 186th Inf. Bde.
6. 8th Bn West Yorkshire Regt.
7. 2/4th Bn. Duke of Wellington's Regt.
8. Left Flank Bn.
9. M.G.C.
10. 186th T.M.B.
11. Rear H.Q.
12. Details.
13. File.
14. War Diary.

Appendix 2.

2/7th BN DUKE OF WELLINGTON'S REGIMENT.   Copy No...

Operation Order No 25.
---oOoOoOo---

Ref. Map 57.d.N.E.

1. The Battalion will be relieved in the PURPLE SYSTEM by the 2/4th Bn Duke of Wellington's Regiment on night June 6th/7th.

2. Companies will be relieved by the same lettered Companies of 2/4th Bn Duke of Wellington's Regt. Order of relief will be 'B' Coy. 'C', 'A', 'D', H.Q. Coy.

3. 5 guides per Company and 2 from H.Q. will rendezvous on road at E.17.a.5.5. at 9 p.m. Guides will have written instructions. Lieut E.W.Taylor will be in charge of the guides and will meet them at the rendezvous.

4. An advance party from 2/4th Bn Duke of Wellington's Regt will report to Companies on the morning of the 6th June.

5. All trench stores, work in hand etc, will be carefully handed over. A list of stores to be handed over will be forwarded to H.Q. by noon to-morrow.

6. Completion of relief will be reported by code word 'WATER'.

7. On completion of relief, the Battalion will move into VALLEY CAMP, and be in Brigade Reserve.

8. Route :- ESSARTS-HALMSBOAMP - thence by track to BIENVILLERS-SOUASTRE Road.

9. Lieut A.Tanner., M.C. will take over the new Camp at noon on June 6th. He will arrange guides for Companies from men at Rear Headquarters, to meet the Battalion on the SOUASTRE-BIENVILLERS Road just outside S SOUASTRE.

10. All mess-boxes, spare stores, petrol tins etc will be dumped on ration dump by 9 p.m. Transport Officer will arrange to collect. Limbers for Lewis Guns, will meet Companies on road at E.17.a.5.5. Care will be taken that all petrol tins are taken down.

11. Arrival in new Camp will be notified to Headquarters as soon as possible.

12. ACKNOWLEDGE.

Ernest W Taylor. Lieut
for Capt & Adjt
5.6.1918.   2/7th Bn Duke of Wellington's Regt.

Copies to :-   1 to 4.   O's C Companies.
              5.   186th Inf. Bde.
              6.   2/4th Bn Duke of Wellington's Regt.
              7.   8th Bn West Riding Regt.
              8.   1st Bn Welsh Guards.
              9.   Details.
              10.   File.
              11.   War Diary.
              12.   Rear H.Q.

Copy No. 9......

2/7th. BN. DUKE OF WELLINGTON'S REGIMENT.
Operation Order No. 59.

1. The Battalion will relieve the 5th. K.O.Y.L.I. in the line to-morrow, June 10th.

2. On completion of relief, Companies will be disposed as under:-
   - 'C' Company.   Right Front.
   - 'A'   "   Left Front.
   - 'D'   "   Support.
   - 'B'   "   Support.

3. Companies will relieve as under:-
   - 'A' Coy. 2/7th. will relieve 'A' Coy. 5th. K.O.Y.L.I.
   - 'B' "   "   "   "   'D' "   "   "
   - 'C' "   "   "   "   'C' "   "   "
   - 'D' "   "   "   "   'B' "   "   "

4. An Advance Party of 1 Officer per Company and 1 N.C.O. per Platoon will report to Headquarters 5th. K.O.Y.L.I. at 9.30 p.m. to-night.

5. Platoon Guides and two for Battalion Headquarters will be at K.23.c.25.95. at 9.30 p.m.

6. Order of march :- 'A' Coy, 'C', 'D', 'B', H.Q.Coy
   The first Company will leave VALLEY CAMP at 8.30 p.m.
   The usual distances will be maintained.

7. Route will be :- CAMP - SOUASTRE-BIENVILLERS ROAD - WILLOW PATCH TRACK - LA BRAYELLE ROAD - POPLAR.

8. All Trench Stores and work in hand will be carefully taken over. A List of such stores will be forwarded to Battalion Headquarters by 12 noon on 11th. instant.

9. Company Limbers will report to Companies at 7.30 p.m.

10. Completion of relief will be reported by code phrase "CAN YOU INCREASE WATER".

11. Limbers will be unloaded at Company Headquarters except 'A' Company's, which will be unloaded at CRUCIFIX.

12. ACKNOWLEDGE.

                                    Captain & Adjutant,
                                    2/7th. Bn. Duke of Wellington's Regiment.

9.6.18.

Copies to :-   1 to 4. Os.C.Companies.
                  5.   5th. K.O.Y.L.I.
                  6.   186th. Inf. Bde.
                  7.   Details.
                  8.   File.
                  9.   War Diary.

SECRET   Appendix 4
                                                         Copy No. 11

        2/7th Bn Duke of Wellington's Regt
              Operation Order No 30

1. The Battalion will be relieved in the Line
by the 2/4th Bn Duke of Wellington's Regt on night
June 14/15th.

2. Companies will be relieved as follows:-
    "A" Coy 2/7th D/W's Regt by "C" Coy 2/4th D of W's Regt
    "B" -   "D"
    "C" -   "B"
    "D" -   "A"

3. One guide per Coy and 2 guides from B.H.Q.
will rendezvous at H.Q. 2/4th D. of W's Regt
at 10 PM.
        These guides will have written instructions.
        Platoon guides will be arranged as follows:-
LEFT Front Coy:- The advance H.Q. of 2/4th D of W. will act as such
and will meet incoming Coy at L.2.a.95.95 (Coy HQ)
RIGHT Front Coy:- The advance H.Q. of 2/4 D/W's will act as such
and will meet incoming Coy at F.25.c.0.8 (present B.H.Q.)
SUPPORT Coy:- The advance H.Q. of Sp Coy 2/4 D/W's will act as such
and will meet incoming Coy at L.2.a.35.20 (Junction of
CROSS Ave and KENNET)
RESERVE Coy:- will find 4 platoon guides to meet incoming
Coy at F.25.c.0.8. Present B.H.Q.

-1-

3. Coy Commanders will take steps to ensure that all guides and advance N.C.Os of 2/4th D of W's Regt are acquainted with the route.

4. (a) An advance party of 1 Offr and 1 N.C.O per platoon will report to A, C and D Coys tonight.
   (b) An advance party of 1 Offr and 1 N.C.O per platoon will report to 'B' Company at 10 A.M. 14/6/18

5. All Trench Stores, work in hand etc will be carefully handed over. Lists of such stores will be forwarded to HQ by 11 am 14/6/18

6. Completion of relief will be reported by code please "Bi-carbonate of Soda wanted"

7. On completion of relief Battalion will move into the area vacated by 2/4th Bn D of W's Regt and will be in Brigade Reserve.

8. Coys will take over the positions vacated by the Coys of the 2/4th D of W's Regt as follows:-
   'A' Coy 2/7th will take over position vacated by 'C' Coy 2/4th
   'B'   —   —   —   —   —   'D'   —
   'C'   —   —   —   —   —   'B'   —
   'D'   —   —   —   —   —   'A'   —

-2-

7. Coys. will send an advance party of 1 Offr and 1 NCO per platoon to report at H.Q. 2/4th D of W. Regt at 10 hrs 14/6/18

8. Coys. will arrange for guides to be found from the advance party to meet them after relief and guide them to their new position.

9. All trench stores etc will be carefully taken over and lists sent to H.Q. as early as possible 15/6/18

10. Arrival in new positions will be reported by Code word 'LANDED'

11. Rations will arrive at new dumps about 1.30 hrs night 15/16th June.

12. ACKNOWLEDGE

Geo Hattersley
2/Lt & A/Adjt
2/4th Bn Duke of Wellington's Regt

13.6.18

Copies to:— 1 to 4 Dvl Coys   11 War Diary
            5   186 Inf Bde   12 File
            6   2/4th Bn D of W Regt
            7   Right Bn
            8   Left Bn
            9   MGC
            10   Rear HQ

Appendix 5   App. No 12

2/4th The Duke of Wellington's Regt
Operation Order No 31

1. The Battalion will be relieved in the
support line on night 15/16 June
by the 2/4th Hants Regt.

2. [Battalion of 2/4th Hants Regt will
relieve corresponding companies of
2/4th D.of W. — i.e. A Coy will
relieve A Coy.]

3. One guide per Coy [area] will be
sent to [report to?] the night[?] with
that [of the 2/4th?] ahead[?] with[?] [of]
HQ.
These guides will [meet?] up [the?]
[new?] 2/4th Hants Regt at the
junction of STAR [Trench?] and [Rue?]
LA BRAYELLE Rd (E.23.d.1.3) at
which point platoon guides [will?]
lead them to [Trench of?] Platoon
guide will [be made?] [to?]
all guides will [have to?]
[instructions?]

4. [Route to be taken by Coy guides
from SOUASTRE will be...]

4. (Continued)
SOUASTRE – HENU WILLERS Road –
Willow PATCH Wood – POPLAR – to
junction of & N BRAWELLE Road
old STAFF Trench (E.13.d.3.6)

5. On arrival of full Relief Coy will
leave SOUASTRE by Platoon, first
platoon leaving at 8.45 p.m.

6. Advance party of 24th Manch. Regt
will report with Bn tomorrow
tonight.

7. All defence schemes, indents,
reports & other maps and Report
store will be carefully handed over.
Lists of above will be forwarded to
HQ by 11 a.m. 15.6.18.

8. Completion of relief will be
reported by code word "Solution
arrived".

9. On completion of relief Companies
will march to SOUASTRE and will
be conveyed from there to AMPLIER
by bus.

-2-

10. Instructions ref Lewis Guns and
Stokes Mor A.A. will be issued
later

11. ACKNOWLEDGE.

Geo. Hattersley
Lt & Adjt
2/7th Bn Duke of Wellington Regt

14.6.16.

Copies to   1 to 4   A B C Companies
            5   1/6th Infy Bde
            6   2/4th Bn Yorks Regt
            7   Right Bn
            8   Left Bn
            9   MGC
            10   Details
            11   Rear HQ
            12   War Diary
            13   -ditto-
            14   File